D1580752

Power
Eating and
Fitness
Log

Susan M. Kleiner, Ph.D.,R.D.
and
Melody Biringer

The *Power Eating and Fitness Log* was inspired by the book *Power Eating,* by Dr. Susan M. Kleiner, published in 1998 from Human Kinetics Publishers, Inc. *Power Eating,* is available from the publishers toll-free at **1-800-747-4457** or at their website, http://www.humankinetics.com/

Other books by Dr. Susan Kleiner:

High-Performance Nutrition. The total eating plan to maximize your workout.

The Be Healthier, Feel Stronger Vegetarian Cookbook

The High Performance Cookbook

The information contained in this book is not intended to serve as a replacement for the advice of a physician. Any use of the information set forth in this book is at the reader's discretion. The authors specifically disclaim any and all liability arising directly from the use or application of any information contained in this book. A health care professional should be consulted prior to following any new diet or exercise program.

Table of Contents

Daily Logs

Forward

I am in my mid 30's but since my teenage years most of my life has been spent yo-yo dieting. This madness started with a $50 bet with my family on who could lose 10 pounds the fastest. Growing up in a family which didn't exercise but deprived themselves of food, I've tried all the diets: Scarsdale, Cambridge, Topfast (a liquid diet), Jenny Craig, Weight Watchers, Phen Phen, Redux and very low calorie diets. They all worked, yet that lifestyle of up 10, down 10, up 20, down 15, took its toll until my late 20's where I was fifty pounds up! For the first time in my life, I also started having weight related problems, including gallbladder attacks, then high cholesterol, and low self-esteem. To compound my dilemma, I own a gourmet food company where the scent of freshly baked goods tempts me daily.

By then I was resolved to figure out how to live a happy, healthy life while not feeling deprived and maintaining a size 8. So, I joined a gym and started an aerobic class three days a week. In the past I'd always start walking in the spring then quit by summer as my business was my priority. Determined to break this self-defeating cycle, I hung on for 6 months maintaining my 3 days a week exercise regimen. I was still discouraged with the results, yet I couldn't turn back.

I read and learned about the benefits of strength training and added it to my regimen. A personal trainer created a program for me and added a variety of aerobic activities like walking, jogging, and hiking. Finally, while continuing to diet and exercise I started to see results in my body, I was feeling strong, a new sensation for me, and I liked it! Now, after 6 years of exercising 6 days a week, I am positively addicted and will be for life!

Yet I still did not feel in control of my eating habits. Although I knew basic nutrition, good choices still didn't come naturally. I wanted my eating to become natural, be nutritionally balanced, yet could I ever not feel deprived? At this point I hired a nutritionist, who created a program with foods I enjoyed so that I could maintain my weight and stop the dreaded yo-yo effect.

Power *Eating* and **Fitness Log**

My choice for a nutritionist was Dr. Susan Kleiner, who I read about in Shape magazine, and I discovered lived in my area. During my consultation with Dr. Kleiner, she showed me how many portions of each food group I should consume daily. Food group balance was the main issue. Starting a food diary with my new nutrition plan was next.

I soon discovered it was still difficult to know what I should be eating and how much. Just cramming my food intake in the note section of a fitness log didn't work. Using the food pyramid, I created a visual guide, crossing out the portions and types of food I had throughout the day. This type of visual recording provides a constant self awareness, and ability to control and direct my daily food choices. I now had a tool that was user-friendly, tracked my progress and showed whether I was in balance.

As a result I've maintained my goal of wearing a size 8 for a year. In the process I've learned that my dress size isn't the issue. The real challenge is - Balance in nutrition, physical health, and spiritual well being.

I have control on this troublesome area of my life as well as a tool to keep me on track. My hope is that I can share this tool with you, and that we both acquire that balance that makes our lives rich.

Melody Biringer

Power *Eating* and **Fitness Log**

Why Keep a Log?

Want to feel stronger and healthier? Want to look better and stay younger? Then you need to sign yourself in to the *Power Eating and Fitness Log*.

Your world today is full of health and diet information. You see it on TV, listen to it on talk radio, read it in books, magazines, newspapers, and on the internet. You have more access to information than ever before. Then why is it still so hard to achieve diet and fitness success?

Disregarding the fact that much of the information out there is unscientifically-based mumbo jumbo, even the good stuff is hard to put into action. It's not enough to learn about it, read about it, think about it, or talk about it. Resoundingly, successful dieters claim that the most important thing that they did to ensure their success was to write down what they ate and how they exercised every day.

This little piece of information is even supported by scientific research. We know that when people keep records of what they eat every day, they eat more healthfully, lose more weight and are more successful at keeping that weight off. And if they happen to put on a few pounds, they can go right back to recording their food and easily lose the weight again.

If gaining muscle and strength is your goal, there is no better example than championship bodybuilders. They all keep records of their daily routines, weekly goals, and monthly outcomes.

It's time to face the music. There are no excuses left. *Power Eating* gives you the most cutting-edge information about what to do with your diet and exercise to make you leaner, stronger, have more energy, look better and be healthier. The *Power Eating and Fitness Log* is your guide on how to get there. It's a winning combination.

How to use the Power Eating and Fitness Log

The *Power Eating and Fitness Log* is designed to follow the *Power Eating* diet plan using various recording methods. You don't need to use all of the recording methods. Choose the style that works best for you.

The log is broken up into days and weeks. Each week ends with a weekly recap. Each 4 week period ends with a 4-week recap, and the Log ends with a final, 12-week recap. The recaps allow you to evaluate how you have been doing during each period of time. You can identify where your diet and exercise strengths and weaknesses are, and make a goal plan for the following period of time.

The daily log sheets have several recording styles. Since *Power Eating* is based on 7 food groups (bread/starch, other carbohydrates, fruit, vegetable, protein, dairy, and fats), there is a food group pyramid where you can just visually cross off your servings from the food groups that you have eaten each day. Since fluids are such an important part of the *Power Eating* plan, water makes up the foundation of the food group pyramid. To individualize the pyramid for your personal *Power Eating* plan, adjust the number of servings from each food group by blacking out or drawing in additional serving icons.

Rather than recording what you ate in general food group terms, you might prefer to record your food intake by writing down everything that you've had to eat and drink all day. Each daily log sheet also has a place to record when you ate, what and how much you ate, why you ate, and the calories and fat grams for each food or meal. This style of recording can also be compared to the *Power Eating* food plan.

Since diet is only half of the *Power Eating and Fitness* plan, each day also has a place to record your exercise, including aerobic activity, strength training, and flexibility/stress relaxation. And since the bottom line of any program is ultimately how you feel, there is a place to record that, as well.

Any type of record or log is always more accurate if you carry it with you and record as you go throughout the day. We've designed this log to be easy to carry with you: in a briefcase, backpack, or purse. So do it. Keep it with you. That way you don't have to try and remember at the end of the day what you ate nearly twelve hours before.

Set yourself up for success. After you design your personalized *Power Eating and Fitness* plan, set small, short term goals first, with a recognition of your ultimate long term goals. Most people cannot successfully go from A to Z in one big leap. By setting small, achievable goals, you will be working toward your larger goal with smaller yet triumphant steps rather than one big leap that falters. For instance, maybe in the first week all you want to accomplish is to understand and remember your personalized diet program. You'd also like to find a good personal strength and conditioning trainer to help design your strength training program. In week two you'd like to be able to follow the program even during your two days of business travel. In week three you want to eat your day's requirements for fruits and vegetables every day. In week four you want to get through the week without missing a day of exercise, and you want to eat only when you are hungry. And so on. By the end of the twelfth week your goal is to lose body fat, increase muscle mass, have more energy throughout the day, and feel altogether better.

Power Eating and Fitness is a lifestyle plan, not a diet that you go on to go off. It takes time and commitment to change lifestyle. But it is the most proven way to accomplish your goals now, and for the rest of your life. Unless you see yourself as successful, you'll never stick to your program. So setting smaller goals that you know you can achieve in a shorter period of time will ensure that you reach your ultimate target: feeling stronger and healthier, and looking better and younger. Believe me, it won't take you long. You are already on your way!

Know Your Numbers

The healthiest diet is packed with a variety of foods. By planning your diet based on the number of servings that you need to eat from all of the food groups you will automatically eat a healthy, well-rounded diet. Depending on whether you want to maintain, gain or lose weight, the body has slightly different needs. The following chart has already taken those needs into consideration.

Food Groups	Calories 1,600*	1,800	2,200	2,600	3,000	3,400
Bread, Cereal, Rice & Pasta Group / And other carbohydrates	3/1	6/4	6/3	6/8	8/10	10/9
Fruit Group	3	4	4	6	6	7
Vegetable Group	4	5	4	4	4	4
Milk, Yogurt & Cheese Group	1	1	2	2	2	2
Meats, Poultry, Fish, Dry Beans, Eggs & Nuts Group Very Lean Lean Medium-fat	6 lean 0 med. fat	3 lean 3 med. fat	4 lean 4 med. fat	5 lean 5 med. fat	6 lean 6 med. fat	7 lean 6 med. fat
Fats & Oils	2	3	3	5	6	7
Supplements Gatorade	1 (8 oz.)	1 (8 oz.)	1 (8 oz.)	2 (16 oz.)	3 (24 oz.)	3 (24 oz.)
Kleiner's Muscle Building Formula	1/2 recipe	1 recipe	1 recipe	1 recipe	1 recipe	1 recipe

* Active people should follow this low calorie diet for only 2 weeks.

Know Your Portions

A portion is the amount of food used to determine the numbers of servings for each food group. It is not always the amount of food that you would think of as a serving that you would eat. For example, one portion of pasta is just a half cup. But if you would serve yourself pasta for dinner, you would likely eat at least one cup. One cup of pasta equals 2 servings from the breads and cereals food group.

Learning the portion sizes for servings is the foundation of success. It is the way that calorie control is built into the plan. If you are eating portions that are too large or too small, the plan will not work. Look at the following chart for a listing of foods and serving sizes for each food group. In the beginning you will need to refer to this chart frequently. You should also weigh and measure foods in the beginning, so that you get a handle on the true portion sizes. After a few weeks, you'll be able to do it on your own. Use the charts on the following pages to learn more about portion sizes.

Chart of food groups and serving sizes

Milk, Yogurt and Cheese Group	Fruit Group	Bread, Cereal, Rice and Pasta Group
A portion contains 90 to 120 calories Each portion contains 0 - 3 grams of fat	*A portion contains 60 calories* Each portion contains 0 grams of fat	*Each portion has 60 to 100 calories* Each portion contains 0-1 grams of fat
Food size of one portion	**Food** size of one portion	**Food** size of one portion
Skim milk, or plain nonfat yogurt..........1 cup	Most Fruits, whole ....1 medium	Bread ....1 slice
Evaporated skim milk ....1 cup	Most fruits, chopped or canned in own juice .... $\frac{1}{2}$ cup	Pita ....1 oz.
Nonfat dry milk .... $\frac{1}{3}$ cup	Melon, diced ....1 cup	Bagel, English muffin, bun...................... $\frac{1}{2}$ small (1 oz.)
Nonfat or lowfat soy or rice milk fortified with calcium and vitamins A&D ...1 cup	Berries, cherries, grapes (whole) .... $\frac{3}{4}$ cup	Roll..................................1 small
Buttermilk ....1 cup	Fruit juice .... $\frac{1}{2}$ cup	Cooked rice, cooked pasta..................... $\frac{1}{2}$ cup
Lowfat or nonfat cottage cheese.................. $\frac{1}{2}$ cup	Banana ....1 small	Tortilla....................6-inch round
Ricotta cheese ....2 oz.	Grapefruit, mango .... $\frac{1}{2}$	Crackers ....3-4 small or 2 large
Hard cheese, lowfat or nonfat (cheddar, Swiss).....................1 oz.	Plums...................................2 ea.	Croutons .... $\frac{1}{3}$ cup.
American cheese ....1 slice	Apricots ....4 ea.	Pretzels, nonfat chips............1 oz.
Lowfat or nonfat ice cream or frozen yogurt .... $\frac{1}{2}$ cup	Strawberries (whole) ....1 $\frac{1}{4}$ cup	Rice cakes ....2 ea.
Lowfat or nonfat fruit flavored yogurt ....1 cup	Kiwi ....1 ea.	Cooked cereal .... $\frac{1}{2}$ cup
Pudding, lowfat or nonfat.......................... $\frac{1}{2}$ cup	Prunes, dates ....3 ea.	Cold cereal, unsweetened....1 cup
	Figs.......................................2 ea.	Granola................................ $\frac{1}{4}$ cup
	Raisins ....2 Tbs.	Corn, green peas, mashed potato.................. $\frac{1}{2}$ cup
	Juice - Cranberry, grape, prune, fruit blends (100% juice)...................... $\frac{1}{3}$ cup	White or sweet potato baked with skin ....1 small
	Cranberry juice cocktail (reduced calorie).................1 cup	

Chart of food groups and serving sizes - cont.

Meats, Poultry, Fish, Dry Beans, Eggs & Nuts Group

Each Protein portion contains 35 to 75 calories.
Very lean = 35 calories - 0-1 grams of fat
Lean = 55 calories - 3 grams of fat
Medium Fat = 75 calories - 5 grams of fat

Food	size of one portion
VERY LEAN	
White meat skinless poultry,	.1 oz.
White fish	1 oz.
Fresh or canned tuna in water	1 oz.
All shellfish	1 oz.
Beans, peas, and lentils *	½ cup.
Cheeses and processed sandwich meat with 1 gram of fat	1 oz.
Egg white	1 ea.
LEAN:	
Select or Choice grades of lean beef, pork, lamb or veal trimmed of fat	1 oz.
Dark meat skinless poultry or white meat chicken with skin	1 oz.
Oysters, salmon, catfish, sardines, tuna canned in oil	1 oz.
Processed sandwich meat with 3 grams of fat	1 oz.
Parmesan cheese	1 oz.
MEDIUM FAT: Most styles of beef, pork, lamb, veal -trimmed of fat, dark meat poultry with skin	1 oz.
Ground turkey or chicken	1 oz.
Cheese with 5 grams of fat	oz.
Cottage cheese 4.5% fat	1 oz.
Whole egg	1
Regular soy milk	1 cup
Tempeh	¼ cup
Tofu	4 oz. or ½ cup

* Equivalent to 1 very lean meat and 1 bread serving.

Fats & Oils

An Extra portion contains 45 calories
Each portion contains 5 grams of fat

Food	size of one portion
Oil, butter, margarine, full-fat mayonnaise	1 tsp.
Diet Margarine	2 tsp.
Cream cheese, whipped cream, sour cream	1 Tbs.
Cream cheese, whipped cream, sour cream (lowfat or nonfat)	2 Tbs.
Salad dressing (full-fat)	1 Tbs.
Salad dressing (low-fat)	2 Tbs.
Avocado	1/8 medium
Olives	8
Nuts	6-10
Seeds	1 Tbs.
Peanut butter and other nut butters	2 tsp.

Vegetable Group

A portion contains 25 calories
Each portion contains 0 grams of fat

Food	size of one portion
Most cooked vegetables	½ cup
Most raw leafy vegetables	1 cup
Sprouts	1 cup
Most other raw vegetables, chopped or sliced	1 cup
Vegetable juice	6 oz.
Vegetable soup	1 cup
Tomato sauce	½ cup
Salsa (made without oil)	3 Tbs.

Other Carbohydrates

Each serving of other carbohydrates contains the equivalent of 15 grams of carbohydrate. Some foods listed are more than 1 serving. You can substitute or exchange these foods for each other based on the number of servings.

Food	size of one portion	Number of Servings
Angel food cake, unfrosted	1/12" cake	2
Hard candy	3 small	1
Cookie, fat-free	2 small	1
Cranberry sauce, jellied	1/4 cup	1 1/2
Frozen fruit juice bars, 100% juice	1 bar (3 oz.)	1
Fruit snacks, chewy (pureed fruit concentrate)	1 roll (3/4 oz.)	1
Fruit spreads, 100% fruit	1 Tbs.	1
Gatorade thirst quencher	1 cup	1
Gelatin, regular	1/2 cup	1
Gingersnaps	3 small	1
Granola bar, fat-free	1 bar	2
Ice cream, fat-free, no sugar added	1/2 cup	1
Jam or jelly, regular	1 Tbs.	1
Liquor	1 oz.	2
Beer, wine	6 oz. (regular) or 8 oz. (light beer)	1 1
Pudding, regular (made with low-fat milk)	1/2 cup	2
Pudding, sugar-free (made with low-fat milk)	1/2 cup	1
Salad dressing, fat-free	1/4 cup	1
Sherbet, sorbet	1/2 cup	2
Soda pop	12 oz.	3
Syrup, light	2 Tbs.	1
Syrup, regular	1 Tbs.	1
Syrup, regular	1/4 cup	4
Yogurt, frozen, fat-free, no sugar added	1/2 cup	1
Yogurt, non-fat with fruit	1 cup	3
Yogurt, non-fat, no sugar added	1 cup	1 1/2

Fluid Intake

Drink one quart (4 cups) of fluid for every 1,000 calories of food you eat (minimum 8 cups per day). Consume more in hot, humid weather or at high altitude. Avoid caffeine and alcohol, which are dehydrating. Follow these additional guidelines.

• Fluids should be cool.

• For exercise lasting an hour or less, water is sufficient for replacing lost fluids

• If you like flavored drinks better, then use flavored beverages.

• For intense exercise last less than one hour and exercise lasting more than an hour, carbohydrate-electrolyte sport drinks containing 6 to 8 percent carbohydrates (grams per 100 milliliters) are best. Carbohydrates can be glucose, sucrose, or maltodextrins. Fructose should not be the sole or primary carbohydrate, but is acceptable in smaller amounts.

• Drink two cups of water or sports drink two hours before exercise.

• Drink four to six ounces every 15 to 20 minutes during exercise.

• Drink 16 to 20 ounces of fluid for every pound of body weight lost during exercise.

Meal replacers: These are milkshake-type drinks and are good to use as balanced snacks. After exercise, the combination of protein and carbohydrate enhances glycogen replenishment in the muscles. After strength training exercise, carbohydrate and protein combinations potentially enhance muscle building. Meal replacers are great to use on the day of contests to avoid feeling full. There are a number of meal replacer supplements on the market. For a less expensive, homemade version, try Kleiner's Muscle Building Formula. Don't forget to figure the calories, protein, fat, and carbohydrate from these supplements into your dietary allowances.

Kleiner's Muscle-Building Formula

8 ounces skim milk
1 packet Carnation Instant Breakfast
1 banana
1 tablespoon peanut butter
Blend until smooth.

One serving contains:

Nutrients	Food Group Servings
438 calories	1 milk serving
70 grams carbohydrate	3 other carbohydrate servings
17 grams protein	1/2 lean meat serving
10 grams fat	1 fat serving
	1 fruit serving

Vitamins and Mineral Supplements

A daily antioxidant multivitamin/mineral tablet is recommended, especially for women or those following the 1,600 calorie diet.

Vitamin E: 100 to 400 IU supplement is recommended.

Calcium: Men and women who avoid dairy products due to taste or physical discomfort should take 800 to 1,200 milligrams a day. It is best to try to get as much calcium as possible from food. Supplementation is also recommended for diets under 2,200 calories.

Creatine: If you are trying to seriously build muscle and you have already perfected your diet and training regimen, this supplement is worth a try. If you are a partial or full vegetarian, it may make a considerable difference since creatine is found naturally in meat. See the book *Power Eating* for a more extensive discussion.

Set a Goal

Choose Your Goal

To design an eating plan based on your personal needs, you must first determine your healthy body weight. What is healthy body weight? It is the body weight and body composition (muscle vs. fat) where you look good, feel great, and perform better. More important, your healthy body weight is where you'll have the lowest risk of heart disease, stroke, diabetes, hypertension, cancer, and other weight-related problems. The following section describes methods for determining healthy body weight and healthy body composition. Choose the ones that feel most comfortable to you. Some people really need to watch a scale. If you do, select another method that will show you body shape changes as well. By choosing methods that measure different things, you will have the greatest chance to get a truer picture of what the *Power Eating and Fitness Log* and living can do for your body.

Find Your Healthy Weight

There are a couple of ways to find your healthy body weight. One is a simple calculation designed to identify desirable weight ranges: For men, take 106 lb. for the first 5 ft. of your height, and add 6 lb. for each additional inch to arrive at the midpoint of a healthy weight range. For women, take 100 lb. for the first 5 ft. of your height, and add 5 lb. for each extra inch to get the midpoint of your healthy body weight range. If you fall within 10% on either side (lower or higher) of that midpoint, you're within a healthy weight range. The lower end of the ranges are for small-boned individuals; the upper end , for larger boned people. To make it easy for you, we've provided healthy weight ranges (with midpoints in bold) in the following table. Compare your present weight with the ranges on the healthy weight chart. If you're within a healthy weight range, congratulations. But if you're more than 10% under the lower end of your range, you may be underweight. Ten percent over the upper end of your range is considered overweight. Twenty percent over that upper end may indicate obesity.

Healthy Weight Ranges

Height	Women	Men
4'10"	81-**90**-99	85-**94**-103
4'11"	86-**95**-105	90-**100**-110
5'	90-**100**-110	95-**106**-117
5'1"	95-**105**-116	101-**112**-123
5'2"	99-**110**-121	106-**118**-130
5'3"	104-**115**-127	112-**124**-136
5'4"	108-**120**-132	117-**130**-143
5'5"	113-**125**-138	122-**136**-150
5'6"	117-**130**-143	128-**142**-156
5'7"	122-**135**-149	133-**148**-163
5'8"	126-**140**-154	139-**154**-169
5'9"	131-**145**-160	144-**160**-176
5'10"	135-**150**-165	149-**166**-183
5'11"	140-**155**-171	155-**172**-189
6'	144-**160**-176	160-**178**-196
6'1"	149-**165**-182	166-**184**-202
6'2"	153-**170**-187	171-**190**-209
6'3"	158-**175**-193	176-**196**-216
6'4"	162-**180**-198	182-**202**-222
6'5"	167-**185**-204	187-**208**-229
6'6"	171-**190**-209	193-**214**-235
6'7"	176-**195**-215	198-**220**-242
6'8"	180-**200**-220	203-**226**-249
6'9"		209-**232**-255
6'10"		214-**238**-262

Power *Eating* and **Fitness Log**

Time Your Meals For Best Results

- Eat small, frequent meals to promote calorie burning versus fat storage. Five to six meals a day are best – more if your calories are higher than 3,000 a day. Make sure to eat breakfast if you work out in the morning. You can eat after your workout, but make sure to drink beforehand. Eat smaller meals in the evening. It is best to eat two to three hours before exercise. This meal should be high in carbohydrates and low in fat (except when you are trying to lose fat, when you should avoid carbohydrate before and during your workout).

- Replace your glycogen stores by consuming high-carbohydrate foods within 15 minutes to two hours following exercise.

- Promote muscle building by consuming a carbohydrate-protein formula within two hours following strength training exercise.

Body Weight versus Body Fat

Calculating healthy body weight ranges doesn't tell the whole story. You need to know how much of your weight is body fat. You could be within a healthy range, but undermuscled and overfat. That is not healthy. Or you could be overweight by healthy weight ranges, but be low in body fat and highly muscled and fit. This is a good place to be. A quick way to see whether you're overfat is to pinch the skin two inches above your belly button. If you can pinch more than one inch of skin in that area, you may be overfat.

Finding Your Body Fat Percentage

To set better fitness goals, it helps to know what's optimal in terms of body fat. Healthy ranges of body fat are 22-25 percent for women and 15-20 percent for men. If you're an athlete, it might be desirable to have slightly lower percentages. Technically, you're considered overfat if your body fat percentage exceeds 20% for men and 25% for women.Unfortunately, there's no simple calculation to figure out your fat pounds. A variety of methods can be used to measure and track body composition. The two methods I recommend are skinfold calipers and body circumference measurements. Many gyms and trainers now have access to quicker methods to measure body composition, like bioelectrical impedance. These methods are not very accurate in non-research settings, but they are convenient. As long as you only pay attention to whether you are going up or down, the method is useful. But specific numbers are usually not accurate.

Calculate Your Energy Goal

Now that you have figured out your healthy body weight, you need to decide exactly what your energy goals are. Losing weight and staying in shape depends mostly on "energy balance", but the type of foods you choose to eat also make a difference. If you eat more calories than you expend in daily activities you will gain weight. If you eat fewer calories than you use, you'll lose weight. High fat foods will promote fat gain and inhibit fat loss. High carbohydrate foods are the best sources of energy, and your body prefers to use them as energy rather than store them as fat. To lose a pound of fat you have to create a 3,500 calorie deficit, either by eating less, exercising more, or both. Combining a lower calorie diet with exercise is the best way to go.Here's how to determine the calories you'll need each day to reach your weight goals:

Step 1: Take your healthy body weight and multiply it by 10. This number is the amount of calories you need daily to maintain your heartbeat, breathe, and regulate other basal functions.

Step 2: Select an activity factor from the following table that corresponds to your activity level. Multiply that factor by your healthy body weight.

Step 3: Add the numbers from steps 1 and 2 to arrive at the number of calories you need to eat to lose weight or to maintain weight if you are already at a healthy body weight.

To Gain Weight

Step 4: If you are underweight, or you are trying to gain muscle mass, follow steps 1-3 using your present body weight, and add 500 calories to your total to achieve a healthy weight gain of muscle, rather than body fat.

ACTIVITY FACTORS FOR DETERMINING ENERGY NEEDS

• *Sedentary*: No exercise, gardening or housework

• *Moderately active*: You exercise, garden, do housework 3-5 times a week for 20-30 minutes each time. Also, you use the stairs and walk briskly.

• *Active*: You exercise 3-5 times a week for 60 minutes each session, as well as use stairs and walk briskly.

SEDENTARY	MODERATELY ACTIVE	ACTIVE	VERY ACTIVE	EXTREMELY ACTIVE
3	4	5	7	10

• *Very Active*: You exercise 3-5 times a week for 90-plus minutes each session. Or you do more than one 60-minute workout session a day. Also you use stairs and walk briskly. You may have other daily physical activity as well. Competitive recreational athletes often fit into this category.

• *Extremely Active*: You exercise 5 or more times a week for 120-plus minutes each session. Or you work out more than 90 minutes a day. You use stairs and walk briskly. Professional athletes often fit into this category.

Illustration: Suppose you're a woman whose healthy body weight should be 125 pounds, and you're moderately active. Here's how to figure your daily calories for weight loss:

Step 1: 125 x 10 = 1,250 calories
Step 2: 125 x 4 = 500 calories
Step 3: 1,250 + 500 = 1,750 calories

If this woman was trying to gain weight, and her present body weight was 125 pounds, she would follow steps 1-3, and then do step 4:

Step 4: 1,750 + 500 = 2,250 calories

Training Your Body

If you want to look and feel great, be strong and live young, you need to eat right and train your heart, lungs, and muscles. Except for athletes training to increase their strength or bodybuilders trying to alter their physiques, not many people strength train. But strength training is just as important to your exercise program as aerobic conditioning. The American College of Sports Medicine now recommends that everyone include strength training and conditioning in their regular exercise routine. Not to become muscle-bound, but to stay toned and fit, and maintain your present level of lean muscle mass.

Maintaining muscle mass isn't just important for athletes. It is critical for the maintenance of health and physical function as you age. Scientists used to think that muscle-loss was a natural by-product of the aging process. But now we know that most muscle-loss is due to inactivity. When people participate in resistance training very little muscle is lost over time. People who maintain their muscle mass have less risk of osteoporosis, diabetes, heart disease, and obesity. They are less likely to fall and to fracture bones. And they are more likely to maintain their independence into old age, since they have the strength to walk and care for themselves. They are truly living younger, healthier lives.

When it comes to maintaining body weight and losing body fat, strength training is the key. Muscle is the metabolically active tissue in your body. It's muscle that burns calories; fat just hangs out. So the more muscle that you have, the more calories that you burn, even while you sit there reading this book. The more muscle that you have, the more calories you can eat, the more nutrient-packed and healthy your diet, and you can still lose weight. And strength training and building muscle burns lots of calories.

Ideally, you should design your exercise program to consist of 2 to 3 strength training workouts and 3 to 4 1-hour(minimum) aerobic workouts each week. This will promote the best body shaping results. If you are new to strength training and have never been trained to use weight lifting equipment, ideally you should find a certified strength and conditioning specialist to work with. They use the credentials "CSCS". There are also ways other than lifting weights to strength train. A good trainer will always find the right program for you.

Choose Your Heart Rate Training Zone

The ideal aerobic workout to improve cardiovascular fitness is geared at 70-85% of maximum heart rate. To maximize fat burning, a workout should be targeted at 60-70% of maximum heart rate. To achieve both cardiovascular fitness and fat burning, gear your workouts at 70% of your maximum heart rate.

To generally determine your maximum heart rate use the following age-adjusted formula (if you are older than 40 and very fit, these numbers may be low):

Maximum heart rate (beats per minute) = 226 - your age (for women)
Maximum heart rate (beats per minute) = 220 - your age (for men)

Heart Rate Training Zone Chart

% of Max HR	Wellness Zones	Fuel Used	Description	Energy Expended (calories/min)
90 - 100	Performance Zone	90% Carb 10% Fat 1% Pro	Feel the burn	15 - 20
80 - 90	Performance Zone	85% Carb 15% Fat 1% Pro	Difficult	>15
70 - 80	Fitness Zone	50% Carb 50% Fat 1% Pro	Somewhat hard	>12
60 - 70	Health Zone	10% Carb 85% Fat 5% Pro	Light work	>10
50 - 60	Health Zone	10% Carb 85% Fat 5% Pro	Breaking a sweat	>6
25 - 50	Resting Zone		No exercise	

Chart adapted from: Edwards, Sally: The Heart Rate Monitor Book. Polar Electro, 1992

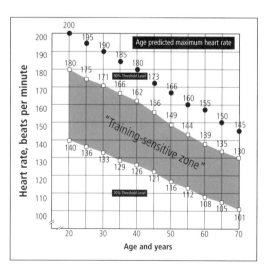

This chart illustrates the maximal heart rates and the training-sensitive zone for use by men and women of different ages.

Cross Training for Variety

The secret to successful fitness is to introduce variety into your exercise program. A well-rounded program will include athletic activities that build your cardiovascular health and develop coordination and balance. To make sure your workouts are well-rounded, use the chart below as a guide to designing the right program for you.

Activity	Cardiovascular	Strength	Flexibility	Coordination/Balance
Walking	•			
Running	•			•
Hiking	•	•		•
Cross-country skiing	•	•		•
Aerobics	•			•
Boxing	•	•		•
Bicycling	•	•		•
Stationary bike	•			
Swimming	•	•	•	•
Tennis	•			•
Stair climbing	•	•		
Slide	•	•		•
Step	•	•		•
Jumping rope	•			•
Basketball	•			•
In-line skating	•	•		•
Volleyball	•			•
Ballet		•	•	•
Ballroom dancing	•			•
Free-weight lifting		•		
Weight machines		•		
Pilate's		•	•	
Yoga		•	•	•
Tai Chi			•	•
Sculling/rowing	•	•	•	•
Rock climbing		•	•	•

Using the Log Pages

The following pages are examples of how you can use the log and the recap pages. We've illustrated some examples of what information you will want to keep track of throughout the weeks ahead. Use these as a guide, but adjust them to meet your lifestyle.

Sample of Daily Log Page

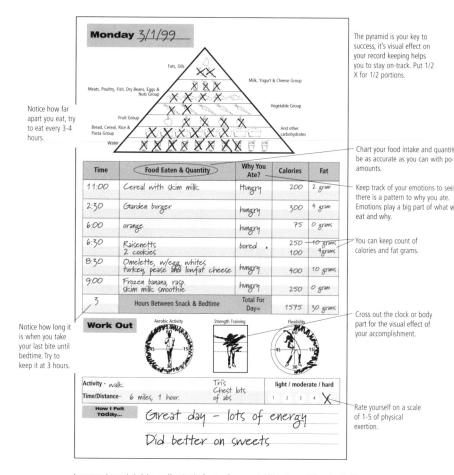

As you complete each day's log, you'll notice the "patterns" you are establishing in your daily routine. You'll be able to summarize your weeks in the -1week, 4 week, and 12 week recaps. The log will become your tool for success. Once your log is full, just order another one from -Get Pumped- to continue your program.

Sample of Weekly Recap Pages

Weekly Recap

Dog ear the weekly and four week recap pages to make it easier to find at the end of each week.

	M	T	W	Th	F	Sat	Sun	★ Good √ Needs Work
Fat	☆	☆	☆	☆	+	X	X	☆
Dairy	☆	☆	☆	–	–	–	–	✓
Protein	☆	☆	☆	☆	☆	☆	☆	☆
Veggies	☆	–	–	☆	☆	☆	☆	☆
Fruits	☆	☆	☆	☆	☆	☆	☆	☆
Breads & Grains	☆	X	☆	☆	☆	☆	☆	☆
Water	☆	☆	☆	☆	☆	–	☆	☆

* = good   + = too much   - = not enough

This is the star system like when your were a kid. Give yourself a star if you hit your goal, or a + or - if you went over or under your ideal numbers. Don't be too hard on yourself. End the week with a star if you did mostly good.

Goals For Next Weeks Fuel:

Watch the fat esp. on weekends, incorporate more dairy.
Keep being creative on veggies
Keep drinking water, add 1 glass a day.

Recap the eating week and make a goal for next week.

	M	T	W	Th	F	Sat	Sun	Total or Average For Week
Time Between Last Snack & Bedtime	.5	1	1	1.5	2	2	.5	1.21
Cardio Sessions	1	1	1	1	–	–	1	5
Strength Training Sessions	1	1	–	1	1	–	–	4
Flexibility	1	1	1	1	1	–	–	5
Abs	1	1	1	1	–	–	1	5
Intensity Level	5	5	5	4.5	3	–	5	4.58
Other miles walked	6		5				2.5	13.5

Add and divide by 7 to get end result.

Record 1 for a session to see how many cardio, strength & flexibility sessions you are accomplishing in a week.

Add and divide by session to get end result.

This is for you to record whatever you want.

Goals For Next Weeks Workout:

Good week – kick up the walking 2-3 more miles next week

Sample of four week recap

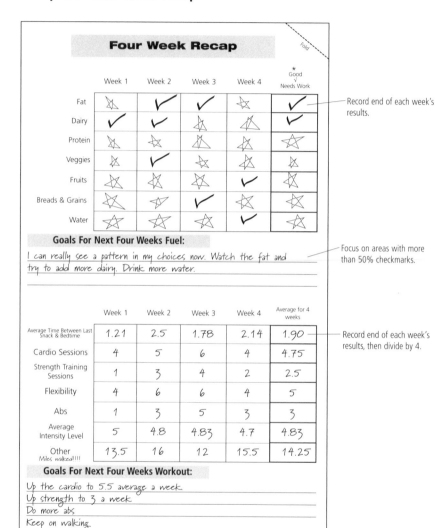

Four Week Recap

	Week 1	Week 2	Week 3	Week 4	★ Good √ Needs Work
Fat	☆	✓	✓	☆	✓
Dairy	✓	✓	☆	☆	✓
Protein	☆	☆	☆	☆	☆
Veggies	☆	✓	☆	☆	☆
Fruits	☆	☆	☆	✓	☆
Breads & Grains	☆	☆	✓	☆	☆
Water	☆	☆	☆	✓	☆

Record end of each week's results.

Goals For Next Four Weeks Fuel:

I can really see a pattern in my choices now. Watch the fat and try to add more dairy. Drink more water.

Focus on areas with more than 50% checkmarks.

	Week 1	Week 2	Week 3	Week 4	Average for 4 weeks
Average Time Between Last Snack & Bedtime	1.21	2.5	1.78	2.14	1.90
Cardio Sessions	4	5	6	4	4.75
Strength Training Sessions	1	3	4	2	2.5
Flexibility	4	6	6	4	5
Abs	1	3	5	3	3
Average Intensity Level	5	4.8	4.83	4.7	4.83
Other Miles walked!!!!	13.5	16	12	15.5	14.25

Record end of each week's results, then divide by 4.

Goals For Next Four Weeks Workout:

Up the cardio to 5.5 average a week
Up strength to 3 a week
Do more abs
Keep on walking

Sample of twelve week recap

Twelve Week Recap

Record end of four week recap here

	End Of Week 4	End Of Week 8	End Of Week 12	Good ★ / Needs Work
Fat	✓	☆	✓	✓
Dairy	✓	☆	☆	☆
Protein	☆	☆	☆	☆
Veggies	☆	✓	✓	✓
Fruits	☆	✓	✓	✓
Breads & Grains	☆	✓	☆	☆
Water	☆	✓	☆	☆

Record end results here. Give yourself a star if you got 2 or more

Fuel Recap:

I really saw my patterns & realized how slow it is to make change, but feel positive I made small changes. Now I think about it subconsciously.

	End Of Week 4	End Of Week 8	End Of Week 12	Average For 12 Weeks
Average Time Between Last Snack & Bedtime	1.90	1.53	1.21	1.55
Cardio Sessions	4.70	5.25	5	5
Strength Training Sessions	25	3	4	3.16
Flexibility	5	5.5	6	5.5
Abs	3	3.75	5	3.91
Average Intensity Level	4.83	4.9	4.66	4.79
Other Miles walked!!!!	14.25	14.5	19	15.91

Add and divide by 3 to get the end result

Workout Recap:

It was fun to track and record my workouts.
The twelve week recap really a gives an "at a glance" summary that provides so much information.

Monday _____

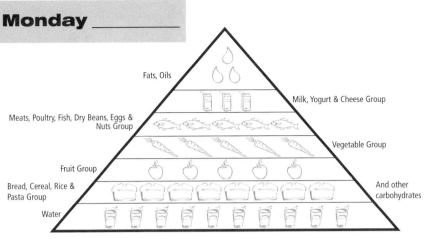

Time	Food Eaten & Quantity	Why You Ate?	Calories	Fat
	Hours Between Snack & Bedtime	Total For Day=		

Work Out

Aerobic Activity

Strength Training

Flexibility

Activity		light / moderate / hard
Time/Distance		1 2 3 4 5

How I Felt Today...

Tuesday _____

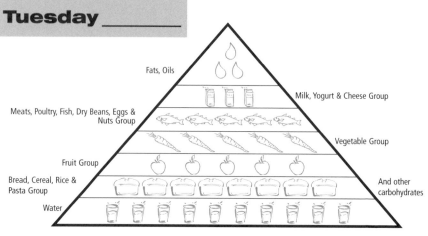

Fats, Oils

Milk, Yogurt & Cheese Group

Meats, Poultry, Fish, Dry Beans, Eggs & Nuts Group

Vegetable Group

Fruit Group

Bread, Cereal, Rice & Pasta Group

And other carbohydrates

Water

Time	Food Eaten & Quantity	Why You Ate?	Calories	Fat
	Hours Between Snack & Bedtime	Total For Day=		

Work Out

Aerobic Activity

Strength Training

Flexibility

Activity	light / moderate / hard
Time/Distance	1 2 3 4 5

How I Felt Today...

Wednesday _____

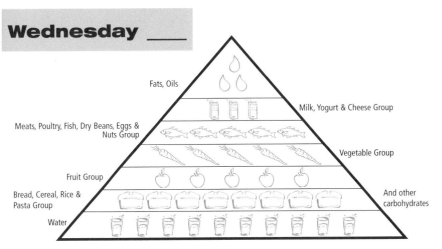

- Fats, Oils
- Milk, Yogurt & Cheese Group
- Meats, Poultry, Fish, Dry Beans, Eggs & Nuts Group
- Vegetable Group
- Fruit Group
- And other carbohydrates
- Bread, Cereal, Rice & Pasta Group
- Water

Time	Food Eaten & Quantity	Why You Ate?	Calories	Fat
	Hours Between Snack & Bedtime	Total For Day=		

Work Out

Aerobic Activity

Strength Training

Flexibility

Activity		light / moderate / hard
Time/Distance		1 2 3 4 5

How I Felt Today...

_____
_____
_____
_____

Thursday _____

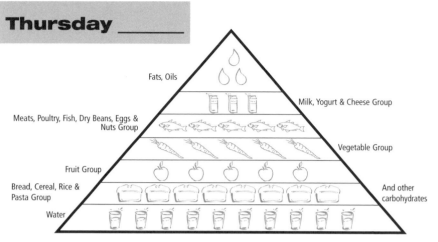

Fats, Oils

Milk, Yogurt & Cheese Group

Meats, Poultry, Fish, Dry Beans, Eggs & Nuts Group

Vegetable Group

Fruit Group

Bread, Cereal, Rice & Pasta Group

And other carbohydrates

Water

Time	Food Eaten & Quantity	Why You Ate?	Calories	Fat
	Hours Between Snack & Bedtime	Total For Day=		

Work Out

Aerobic Activity

Strength Training

Flexibility

Activity

Time/Distance

light / moderate / hard

1   2   3   4   5

How I Felt Today...

_____

_____

_____

_____

Friday _____

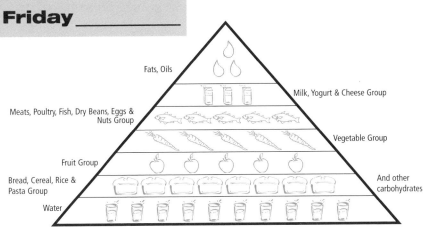

- Fats, Oils
- Milk, Yogurt & Cheese Group
- Meats, Poultry, Fish, Dry Beans, Eggs & Nuts Group
- Vegetable Group
- Fruit Group
- And other carbohydrates
- Bread, Cereal, Rice & Pasta Group
- Water

Time	Food Eaten & Quantity	Why You Ate?	Calories	Fat
	Hours Between Snack & Bedtime	Total For Day=		

Work Out

 Aerobic Activity

Strength Training

 Flexibility

	light / moderate / hard
Activity	
Time/Distance	1 2 3 4 5

How I Felt Today...

Saturday ____

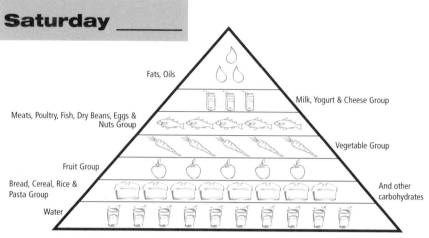

Fats, Oils

Milk, Yogurt & Cheese Group

Meats, Poultry, Fish, Dry Beans, Eggs & Nuts Group

Vegetable Group

Fruit Group

Bread, Cereal, Rice & Pasta Group

And other carbohydrates

Water

Time	Food Eaten & Quantity	Why You Ate?	Calories	Fat
	Hours Between Snack & Bedtime	Total For Day=		

Work Out

Aerobic Activity

Strength Training

Flexibility

Activity	light / moderate / hard
Time/Distance	1 2 3 4 5

How I Felt Today...

_____

_____

_____

_____

Sunday_____

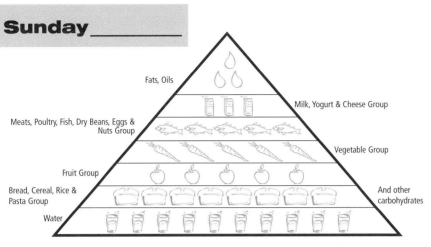

Time	Food Eaten & Quantity	Why You Ate?	Calories	Fat
	Hours Between Snack & Bedtime	Total For Day=		

Work Out

Aerobic Activity

Strength Training

Flexibility

Activity		light / moderate / hard
Time/Distance		1 2 3 4 5

How I Felt Today...

Fold

Weekly Recap

	M	T	W	Th	F	Sat	Sun	* Good √ Needs Work
Fat								
Dairy								
Protein								
Veggies								
Fruits								
Breads & Grains								
Water								

* = good   + = too much   - = not enough

Goals For Next Weeks Fuel:

_____

_____

_____

	M	T	W	Th	F	Sat	Sun	Total or Average For Week
Time Between Last Snack &Bedtime								
Cardio Sessions								
Strength Training Sessions								
Flexibility								
Abs								
Intensity Level								
Other								

Goals For Next Weeks Workout:

_____

_____

_____

Monday _____

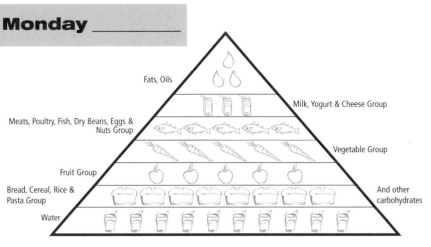

Fats, Oils

Milk, Yogurt & Cheese Group

Meats, Poultry, Fish, Dry Beans, Eggs & Nuts Group

Vegetable Group

Fruit Group

Bread, Cereal, Rice & Pasta Group

And other carbohydrates

Water

Time	Food Eaten & Quantity	Why You Ate?	Calories	Fat
	Hours Between Snack & Bedtime	Total For Day=		

Work Out

Aerobic Activity

Strength Training

Flexibility

Activity	light / moderate / hard
Time/Distance	1 2 3 4 5

How I Felt Today...

Tuesday _____

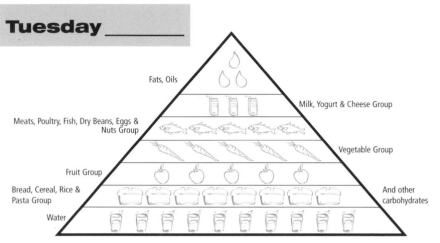

Fats, Oils

Milk, Yogurt & Cheese Group

Meats, Poultry, Fish, Dry Beans, Eggs & Nuts Group

Vegetable Group

Fruit Group

Bread, Cereal, Rice & Pasta Group

And other carbohydrates

Water

Time	Food Eaten & Quantity	Why You Ate?	Calories	Fat
	Hours Between Snack & Bedtime	Total For Day=		

Work Out

Aerobic Activity

Strength Training

Flexibility

Activity _____

Time/Distance _____

light / moderate / hard

1   2   3   4   5

How I Felt Today...

_____
_____
_____
_____

Wednesday ____

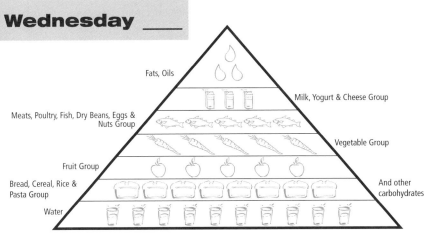

Fats, Oils

Milk, Yogurt & Cheese Group

Meats, Poultry, Fish, Dry Beans, Eggs & Nuts Group

Vegetable Group

Fruit Group

Bread, Cereal, Rice & Pasta Group

And other carbohydrates

Water

Time	Food Eaten & Quantity	Why You Ate?	Calories	Fat
	Hours Between Snack & Bedtime	Total For Day=		

Work Out

Aerobic Activity

Strength Training

Flexibility

Activity

Time/Distance

light / moderate / hard

1   2   3   4   5

How I Felt Today...

Thursday _____

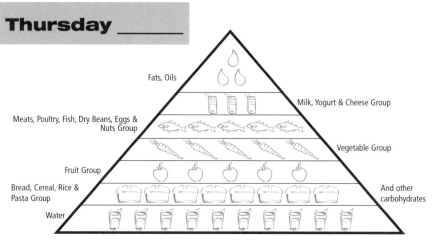

Fats, Oils

Milk, Yogurt & Cheese Group

Meats, Poultry, Fish, Dry Beans, Eggs &
Nuts Group

Vegetable Group

Fruit Group

Bread, Cereal, Rice &
Pasta Group

And other
carbohydrates

Water

Time	Food Eaten & Quantity	Why You Ate?	Calories	Fat
	Hours Between Snack & Bedtime	Total For Day=		

Work Out

Aerobic Activity

Strength Training

Flexibility

Activity	light / moderate / hard
Time/Distance	1 2 3 4 5

**How I Felt
Today...**

Friday _____

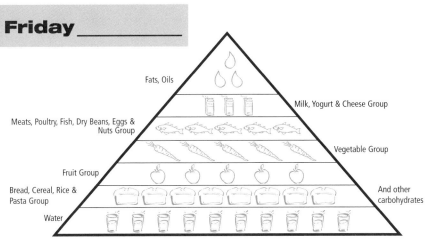

Time	Food Eaten & Quantity	Why You Ate?	Calories	Fat
	Hours Between Snack & Bedtime	Total For Day=		

Work Out

Aerobic Activity

Strength Training

Flexibility

Activity	light / moderate / hard
Time/Distance	1 2 3 4 5

How I Felt Today...

Saturday _____

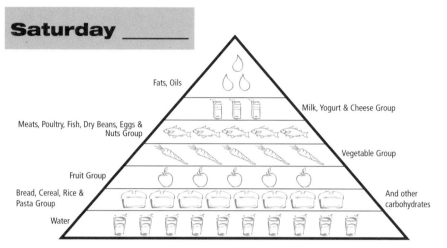

Fats, Oils

Milk, Yogurt & Cheese Group

Meats, Poultry, Fish, Dry Beans, Eggs & Nuts Group

Vegetable Group

Fruit Group

Bread, Cereal, Rice & Pasta Group

And other carbohydrates

Water

Time	Food Eaten & Quantity	Why You Ate?	Calories	Fat
	Hours Between Snack & Bedtime	Total For Day=		

Work Out

Aerobic Activity

Strength Training

Flexibility

Activity	light / moderate / hard
Time/Distance	1 2 3 4 5

How I Felt Today...

Sunday _____

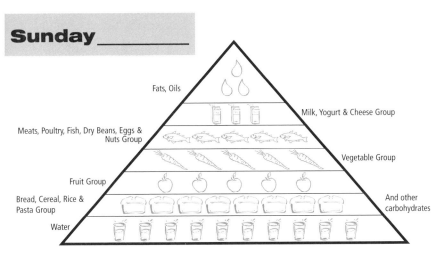

Fats, Oils

Milk, Yogurt & Cheese Group

Meats, Poultry, Fish, Dry Beans, Eggs & Nuts Group

Vegetable Group

Fruit Group

Bread, Cereal, Rice & Pasta Group

And other carbohydrates

Water

Time	Food Eaten & Quantity	Why You Ate?	Calories	Fat
	Hours Between Snack & Bedtime	Total For Day=		

Work Out

Aerobic Activity

Strength Training

Flexibility

Activity _____

Time/Distance _____

light / moderate / hard

1   2   3   4   5

How I Felt Today...

_____
_____
_____
_____

Weekly Recap

	M	T	W	Th	F	Sat	Sun	* Good √ Needs Work
Fat								
Dairy								
Protein								
Veggies								
Fruits								
Breads & Grains								
Water								

* = good   + = too much   - = not enough

Goals For Next Weeks Fuel:

_____

_____

_____

	M	T	W	Th	F	Sat	Sun	Total or Average For Week
Time Between Last Snack &Bedtime								
Cardio Sessions								
Strength Training Sessions								
Flexibility								
Abs								
Intensity Level								
Other								

Goals For Next Weeks Workout:

_____

_____

_____

Monday _____

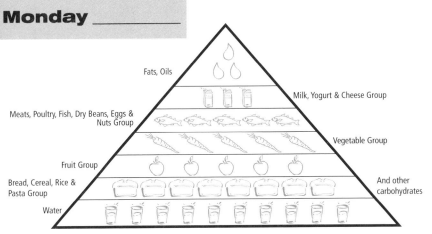

Fats, Oils

Milk, Yogurt & Cheese Group

Meats, Poultry, Fish, Dry Beans, Eggs & Nuts Group

Vegetable Group

Fruit Group

Bread, Cereal, Rice & Pasta Group

And other carbohydrates

Water

Time	Food Eaten & Quantity	Why You Ate?	Calories	Fat
	Hours Between Snack & Bedtime	Total For Day=		

Work Out

Aerobic Activity

Strength Training

Flexibility

Activity	light / moderate / hard
Time/Distance	1 2 3 4 5

How I Felt Today...

_____
_____
_____
_____

Tuesday _____

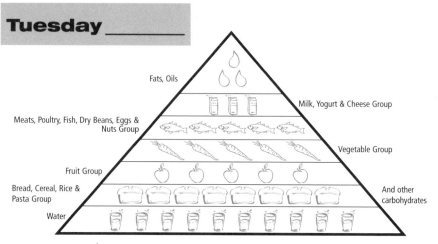

Fats, Oils

Milk, Yogurt & Cheese Group

Meats, Poultry, Fish, Dry Beans, Eggs & Nuts Group

Vegetable Group

Fruit Group

Bread, Cereal, Rice & Pasta Group

And other carbohydrates

Water

Time	Food Eaten & Quantity	Why You Ate?	Calories	Fat
	Hours Between Snack & Bedtime	Total For Day=		

Work Out

Aerobic Activity

Strength Training

Flexibility

Activity		light / moderate / hard
Time/Distance		1 2 3 4 5

How I Felt Today...

Wednesday _____

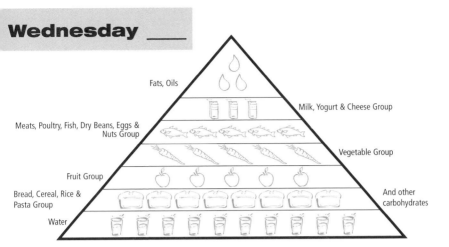

Fats, Oils

Milk, Yogurt & Cheese Group

Meats, Poultry, Fish, Dry Beans, Eggs & Nuts Group

Vegetable Group

Fruit Group

Bread, Cereal, Rice & Pasta Group

And other carbohydrates

Water

Time	Food Eaten & Quantity	Why You Ate?	Calories	Fat
	Hours Between Snack & Bedtime	Total For Day=		

Work Out

Aerobic Activity

Strength Training

Flexibility

Activity	light / moderate / hard
Time/Distance	1 2 3 4 5

How I Felt Today...

Thursday _____

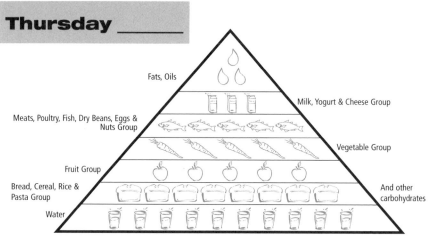

Fats, Oils

Milk, Yogurt & Cheese Group

Meats, Poultry, Fish, Dry Beans, Eggs & Nuts Group

Vegetable Group

Fruit Group

Bread, Cereal, Rice & Pasta Group

And other carbohydrates

Water

Time	Food Eaten & Quantity	Why You Ate?	Calories	Fat
	Hours Between Snack & Bedtime	Total For Day=		

Work Out

Aerobic Activity

Strength Training

Flexibility

Activity	light / moderate / hard
Time/Distance	1 2 3 4 5

How I Felt Today...

Friday _____

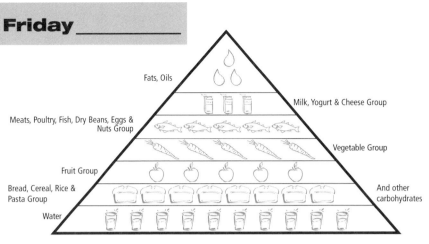

Fats, Oils

Milk, Yogurt & Cheese Group

Meats, Poultry, Fish, Dry Beans, Eggs & Nuts Group

Vegetable Group

Fruit Group

Bread, Cereal, Rice & Pasta Group

And other carbohydrates

Water

Time	Food Eaten & Quantity	Why You Ate?	Calories	Fat
	Hours Between Snack & Bedtime	Total For Day=		

Work Out

Aerobic Activity

Strength Training

Flexibility

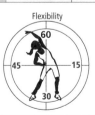

Activity	light / moderate / hard
Time/Distance	1 2 3 4 5

How I Felt Today...

_____

_____

_____

_____

Saturday _____

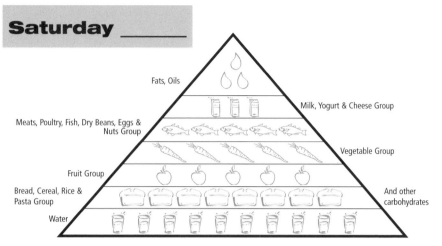

Fats, Oils

Milk, Yogurt & Cheese Group

Meats, Poultry, Fish, Dry Beans, Eggs & Nuts Group

Vegetable Group

Fruit Group

Bread, Cereal, Rice & Pasta Group

And other carbohydrates

Water

Time	Food Eaten & Quantity	Why You Ate?	Calories	Fat
	Hours Between Snack & Bedtime	Total For Day=		

Work Out

Aerobic Activity

Strength Training

Flexibility

Activity	light / moderate / hard
Time/Distance	1 2 3 4 5

How I Felt Today...

Sunday _____

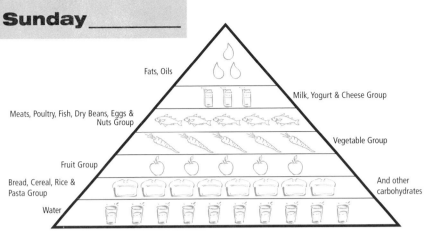

Fats, Oils

Milk, Yogurt & Cheese Group

Meats, Poultry, Fish, Dry Beans, Eggs & Nuts Group

Vegetable Group

Fruit Group

Bread, Cereal, Rice & Pasta Group

And other carbohydrates

Water

Time	Food Eaten & Quantity	Why You Ate?	Calories	Fat
	Hours Between Snack & Bedtime	Total For Day=		

Work Out

Aerobic Activity

Strength Training

Flexibility

Activity	light / moderate / hard
Time/Distance	1 2 3 4 5

How I Felt Today...

Weekly Recap

	M	T	W	Th	F	Sat	Sun	* Good √ Needs Work
Fat								
Dairy								
Protein								
Veggies								
Fruits								
Breads & Grains								
Water								

* = good   + = too much   - = not enough

Goals For Next Weeks Fuel:

_____

_____

_____

	M	T	W	Th	F	Sat	Sun	Total or Average For Week
Time Between Last Snack &Bedtime								
Cardio Sessions								
Strength Training Sessions								
Flexibility								
Abs								
Intensity Level								
Other								

Goals For Next Weeks Workout:

_____

_____

_____

Monday _____

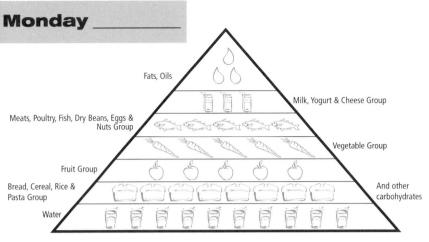

Fats, Oils

Milk, Yogurt & Cheese Group

Meats, Poultry, Fish, Dry Beans, Eggs & Nuts Group

Vegetable Group

Fruit Group

Bread, Cereal, Rice & Pasta Group

And other carbohydrates

Water

Time	Food Eaten & Quantity	Why You Ate?	Calories	Fat
	Hours Between Snack & Bedtime	Total For Day=		

Work Out

Aerobic Activity

Strength Training

Flexibility

Activity		light / moderate / hard
Time/Distance		1 2 3 4 5

How I Felt Today...

_____
_____
_____
_____

Tuesday _____

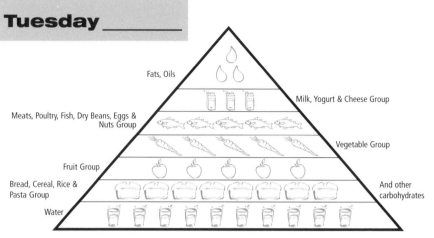

Fats, Oils

Milk, Yogurt & Cheese Group

Meats, Poultry, Fish, Dry Beans, Eggs & Nuts Group

Vegetable Group

Fruit Group

Bread, Cereal, Rice & Pasta Group

And other carbohydrates

Water

Time	Food Eaten & Quantity	Why You Ate?	Calories	Fat
	Hours Between Snack & Bedtime	Total For Day=		

Work Out

Aerobic Activity

Strength Training

Flexibility

Activity	light / moderate / hard
Time/Distance	1 2 3 4 5

How I Felt Today...

Wednesday _____

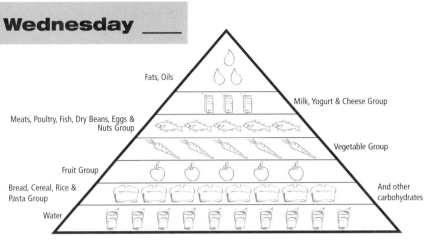

Fats, Oils

Milk, Yogurt & Cheese Group

Meats, Poultry, Fish, Dry Beans, Eggs & Nuts Group

Vegetable Group

Fruit Group

Bread, Cereal, Rice & Pasta Group

And other carbohydrates

Water

Time	Food Eaten & Quantity	Why You Ate?	Calories	Fat
	Hours Between Snack & Bedtime	Total For Day=		

Work Out

Aerobic Activity

Strength Training

Flexibility

Activity	light / moderate / hard
Time/Distance	1 2 3 4 5

How I Felt Today...

Thursday _____

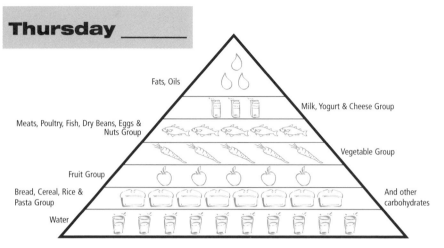

Fats, Oils

Milk, Yogurt & Cheese Group

Meats, Poultry, Fish, Dry Beans, Eggs & Nuts Group

Vegetable Group

Fruit Group

Bread, Cereal, Rice & Pasta Group

And other carbohydrates

Water

Time	Food Eaten & Quantity	Why You Ate?	Calories	Fat
	Hours Between Snack & Bedtime	Total For Day=		

Work Out

Aerobic Activity

Strength Training

Flexibility

Activity	light / moderate / hard
Time/Distance	1 2 3 4 5

How I Felt Today...

_____

_____

_____

_____

Friday _____

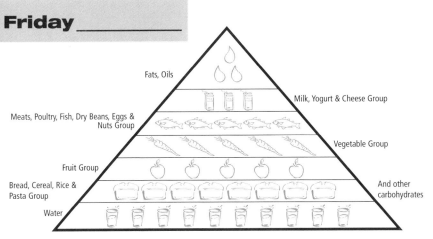

Fats, Oils

Milk, Yogurt & Cheese Group

Meats, Poultry, Fish, Dry Beans, Eggs & Nuts Group

Vegetable Group

Fruit Group

Bread, Cereal, Rice & Pasta Group

And other carbohydrates

Water

Time	Food Eaten & Quantity	Why You Ate?	Calories	Fat
	Hours Between Snack & Bedtime	Total For Day=		

Work Out

Aerobic Activity

Strength Training

Flexibility

Activity	light / moderate / hard
Time/Distance	1 2 3 4 5

How I Felt Today...
_____
_____
_____
_____

Saturday _____

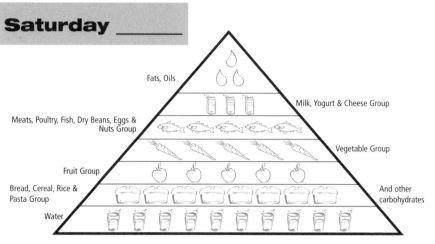

Time	Food Eaten & Quantity	Why You Ate?	Calories	Fat
	Hours Between Snack & Bedtime	Total For Day=		

Work Out

Aerobic Activity

Strength Training

Flexibility

Activity	light / moderate / hard
Time/Distance	1 2 3 4 5

How I Felt Today...

Sunday _____

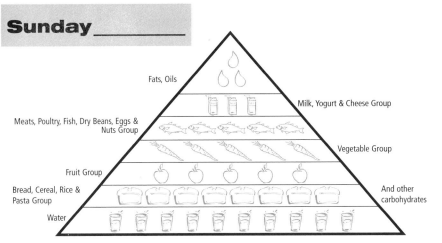

Time	Food Eaten & Quantity	Why You Ate?	Calories	Fat
	Hours Between Snack & Bedtime	Total For Day=		

Work Out

Aerobic Activity

Strength Training

Flexibility

Activity	light / moderate / hard
Time/Distance	1 2 3 4 5

How I Felt Today...

Weekly Recap

	M	T	W	Th	F	Sat	Sun	* Good √ Needs Work
Fat								
Dairy								
Protein								
Veggies								
Fruits								
Breads & Grains								
Water								

* = good   + = too much   - = not enough

Goals For Next Weeks Fuel:

_____

_____

_____

	M	T	W	Th	F	Sat	Sun	Total or Average For Week
Time Between Last Snack &Bedtime								
Cardio Sessions								
Strength Training Sessions								
Flexibility								
Abs								
Intensity Level								
Other								

Goals For Next Weeks Workout:

_____

_____

_____

Four Week Recap

Fold

	Week 1	Week 2	Week 3	Week 4	★ Good √ Needs Work
Fat					
Dairy					
Protein					
Veggies					
Fruits					
Breads & Grains					
Water					

Goals For Next Four Weeks Fuel:

_____

_____

_____

	Week 1	Week 2	Week 3	Week 4	Average for 4 weeks
Average Time Between Last Snack & Bedtime					
Cardio Sessions					
Strength Training Sessions					
Flexibility					
Abs					
Average Intensity Level					
Other					

Goals For Next Four Weeks Workout:

_____

_____

_____

Mindful Quotes

▲ Whatever you can do or dream, you can begin it! For boldness has genius, power and magic in it. Begin it now! —Johann Goethe

▲ Remember, you have it within your power to improve your own health.
— Richard Wolff, MD

▲ Love is not equal to the amount of food your child eats. — Vicki Lansky

▲ I believe that we cannot live better than seeking to become still better than we are.
—- Socrates

▲ We are a nation that thrives on excess, and American nutritional habits have long been based on the premise that "if some is good, more must be better." This may be a fine guideline if the commodity in question is money, love, or sex, but it breaks down like cotton candy when it comes to food and nutrients. — Jane Brody

▲ Only those who will risk going too far can possibly find out how far one can go.
—- T.S. Eliot

▲ It's not the size of the dog in the fight, but the size of the fight in the dog.
— Archie Griffen, two-time Heisman winner (5'9")

▲ I find that the harder I work, the more luck I seem to have. — Thomas Jefferson

▲ Obstacles are those frightful things you see when you take your eyes off your goal.
— Henry Ford

▲ Never leave home starving. Always have a light snack before eating dinner in a restaurant, such as a piece of fruit, a glass of juice, or a carrot.
— Dr. C Everett Koop

▲ Happiness is good health and a bad memory. — Ingrid Bergman

Monday _____

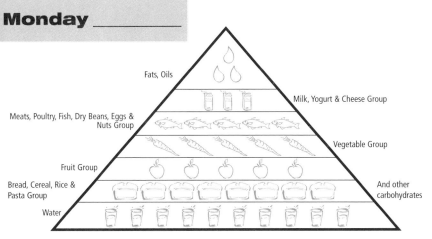

Fats, Oils

Milk, Yogurt & Cheese Group

Meats, Poultry, Fish, Dry Beans, Eggs & Nuts Group

Vegetable Group

Fruit Group

Bread, Cereal, Rice & Pasta Group

And other carbohydrates

Water

Time	Food Eaten & Quantity	Why You Ate?	Calories	Fat
	Hours Between Snack & Bedtime	Total For Day=		

Work Out

Aerobic Activity

Strength Training

Flexibility

Activity _____ **light / moderate / hard**

Time/Distance _____ 1   2   3   4   5

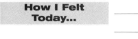
How I Felt Today... _____
_____
_____
_____

Tuesday _____

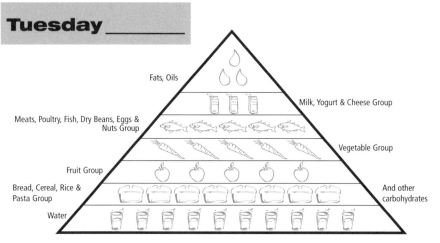

Fats, Oils

Milk, Yogurt & Cheese Group

Meats, Poultry, Fish, Dry Beans, Eggs & Nuts Group

Vegetable Group

Fruit Group

Bread, Cereal, Rice & Pasta Group

And other carbohydrates

Water

Time	Food Eaten & Quantity	Why You Ate?	Calories	Fat
	Hours Between Snack & Bedtime	Total For Day=		

Work Out

Aerobic Activity

Strength Training

Flexibility

Activity	light / moderate / hard
Time/Distance	1 2 3 4 5

How I Felt Today...

_____
_____
_____
_____

Wednesday ____

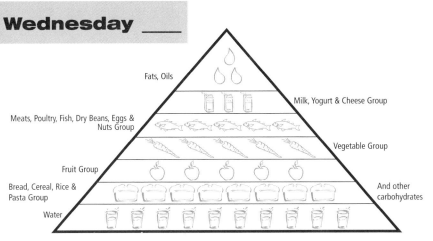

Fats, Oils

Milk, Yogurt & Cheese Group

Meats, Poultry, Fish, Dry Beans, Eggs &
Nuts Group

Vegetable Group

Fruit Group

Bread, Cereal, Rice &
Pasta Group

And other
carbohydrates

Water

Time	Food Eaten & Quantity	Why You Ate?	Calories	Fat
Hours Between Snack & Bedtime		Total For Day=		

Work Out

Aerobic Activity

Strength Training

Flexibility

Activity

Time/Distance

light / moderate / hard

1   2   3   4   5

How I Felt Today...

Thursday _____

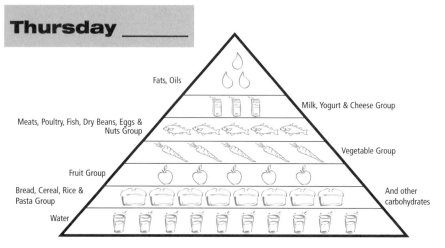

Fats, Oils

Milk, Yogurt & Cheese Group

Meats, Poultry, Fish, Dry Beans, Eggs & Nuts Group

Vegetable Group

Fruit Group

Bread, Cereal, Rice & Pasta Group

And other carbohydrates

Water

Time	Food Eaten & Quantity	Why You Ate?	Calories	Fat
	Hours Between Snack & Bedtime	Total For Day=		

Work Out

Aerobic Activity

Strength Training

Flexibility

Activity	light / moderate / hard
Time/Distance	1 2 3 4 5

How I Felt Today...

Friday _____

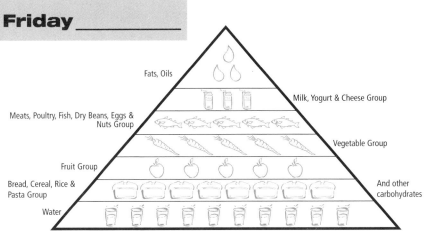

Time	Food Eaten & Quantity	Why You Ate?	Calories	Fat
	Hours Between Snack & Bedtime	Total For Day=		

Work Out

Aerobic Activity

Strength Training

Flexibility

Activity		light / moderate / hard
Time/Distance		1 2 3 4 5

How I Felt Today...

Saturday _____

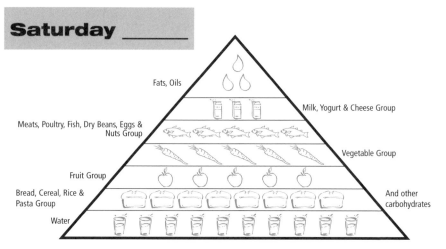

Fats, Oils

Milk, Yogurt & Cheese Group

Meats, Poultry, Fish, Dry Beans, Eggs & Nuts Group

Vegetable Group

Fruit Group

Bread, Cereal, Rice & Pasta Group

And other carbohydrates

Water

Time	Food Eaten & Quantity	Why You Ate?	Calories	Fat
	Hours Between Snack & Bedtime	Total For Day=		

Work Out

Aerobic Activity

Strength Training

Flexibility

Activity	light / moderate / hard
Time/Distance	1 2 3 4 5

How I Felt Today...

_____
_____
_____
_____

Sunday _____

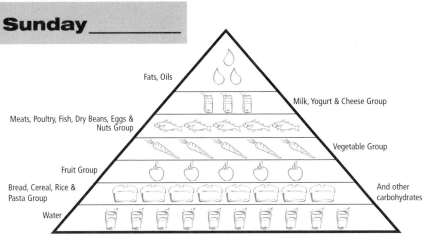

Time	Food Eaten & Quantity	Why You Ate?	Calories	Fat
Hours Between Snack & Bedtime		Total For Day=		

Work Out

 Aerobic Activity

 Strength Training

 Flexibility

Activity	light / moderate / hard
Time/Distance	1 2 3 4 5

How I Felt Today...

Weekly Recap

	M	T	W	Th	F	Sat	Sun	★ Good √ Needs Work
Fat								
Dairy								
Protein								
Veggies								
Fruits								
Breads & Grains								
Water								

★ = good   + = too much   - = not enough

Goals For Next Weeks Fuel:

_____

_____

_____

	M	T	W	Th	F	Sat	Sun	Total or Average For Week
Time Between Last Snack &Bedtime								
Cardio Sessions								
Strength Training Sessions								
Flexibility								
Abs								
Intensity Level								
Other								

Goals For Next Weeks Workout:

_____

_____

_____

Monday _____

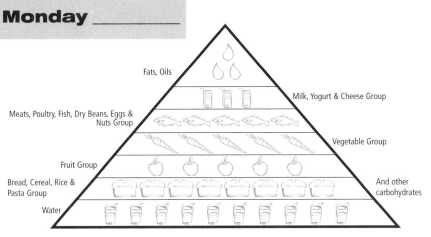

Time	Food Eaten & Quantity	Why You Ate?	Calories	Fat
	Hours Between Snack & Bedtime	Total For Day=		

Work Out

Aerobic Activity

Strength Training

Flexibility

Activity	light / moderate / hard
Time/Distance	1 2 3 4 5

How I Felt Today...

_____
_____
_____
_____

Tuesday _____

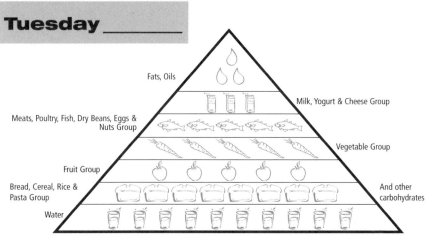

Fats, Oils

Milk, Yogurt & Cheese Group

Meats, Poultry, Fish, Dry Beans, Eggs & Nuts Group

Vegetable Group

Fruit Group

Bread, Cereal, Rice & Pasta Group

And other carbohydrates

Water

Time	Food Eaten & Quantity	Why You Ate?	Calories	Fat
	Hours Between Snack & Bedtime	Total For Day=		

Work Out

Aerobic Activity

Strength Training

Flexibility

Activity	light / moderate / hard
Time/Distance	1 2 3 4 5

How I Felt Today...

Wednesday _____

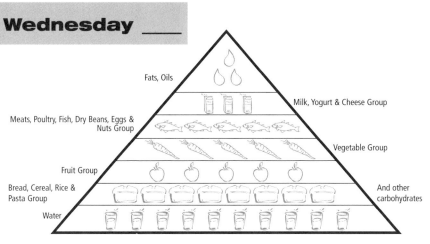

Time	Food Eaten & Quantity	Why You Ate?	Calories	Fat
Hours Between Snack & Bedtime		Total For Day=		

Work Out

Aerobic Activity

Strength Training

Flexibility

Activity	light / moderate / hard
Time/Distance	1 2 3 4 5

How I Felt Today...

Thursday _____

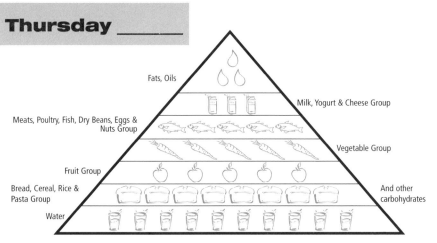

Fats, Oils

Milk, Yogurt & Cheese Group

Meats, Poultry, Fish, Dry Beans, Eggs & Nuts Group

Vegetable Group

Fruit Group

Bread, Cereal, Rice & Pasta Group

And other carbohydrates

Water

Time	Food Eaten & Quantity	Why You Ate?	Calories	Fat
	Hours Between Snack & Bedtime	Total For Day=		

Work Out

Aerobic Activity

Strength Training

Flexibility

Activity	light / moderate / hard
Time/Distance	1 2 3 . 4 5

How I Felt Today...

Friday _____

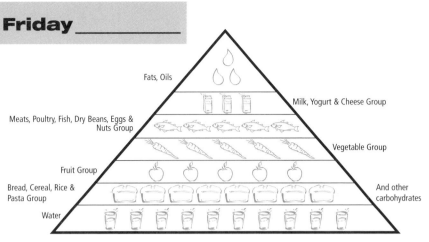

Fats, Oils

Milk, Yogurt & Cheese Group

Meats, Poultry, Fish, Dry Beans, Eggs &
Nuts Group

Vegetable Group

Fruit Group

Bread, Cereal, Rice &
Pasta Group

And other
carbohydrates

Water

Time	Food Eaten & Quantity	Why You Ate?	Calories	Fat
	Hours Between Snack & Bedtime	Total For Day=		

Work Out

Aerobic Activity

Strength Training

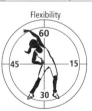

Flexibility

Activity	light / moderate / hard
Time/Distance	1 2 3 4 5

How I Felt Today...

_____
_____
_____
_____

Saturday _____

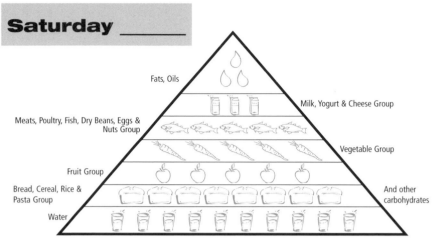

Fats, Oils

Milk, Yogurt & Cheese Group

Meats, Poultry, Fish, Dry Beans, Eggs & Nuts Group

Vegetable Group

Fruit Group

Bread, Cereal, Rice & Pasta Group

And other carbohydrates

Water

Time	Food Eaten & Quantity	Why You Ate?	Calories	Fat
	Hours Between Snack & Bedtime	Total For Day=		

Work Out

Aerobic Activity

Strength Training

Flexibility

Activity	light / moderate / hard
Time/Distance	1 2 3 4 5

How I Felt Today...

_____
_____
_____
_____

Sunday _____

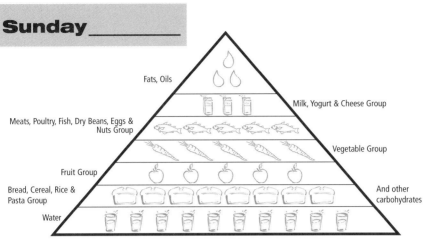

Time	Food Eaten & Quantity	Why You Ate?	Calories	Fat
	Hours Between Snack & Bedtime	Total For Day=		

Work Out

Aerobic Activity

Strength Training

Flexibility

Activity		light / moderate / hard
Time/Distance		1 2 3 4 5

How I Felt Today...

_____
_____
_____
_____

Weekly Recap

	M	T	W	Th	F	Sat	Sun	* Good √ Needs Work
Fat								
Dairy								
Protein								
Veggies								
Fruits								
Breads & Grains								
Water								

* = good   + = too much   - = not enough

Goals For Next Weeks Fuel:

_____

_____

_____

	M	T	W	Th	F	Sat	Sun	Total or Average For Week
Time Between Last Snack &Bedtime								
Cardio Sessions								
Strength Training Sessions								
Flexibility								
Abs								
Intensity Level								
Other								

Goals For Next Weeks Workout:

_____

_____

_____

Monday _____

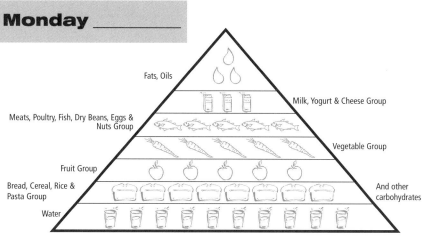

Fats, Oils

Milk, Yogurt & Cheese Group

Meats, Poultry, Fish, Dry Beans, Eggs & Nuts Group

Vegetable Group

Fruit Group

Bread, Cereal, Rice & Pasta Group

And other carbohydrates

Water

Time	Food Eaten & Quantity	Why You Ate?	Calories	Fat
	Hours Between Snack & Bedtime	Total For Day=		

Work Out

Aerobic Activity

Strength Training

Flexibility

Activity		light / moderate / hard
Time/Distance		1 2 3 4 5

How I Felt Today...

Tuesday _____

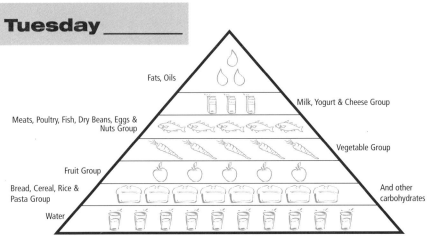

Fats, Oils

Milk, Yogurt & Cheese Group

Meats, Poultry, Fish, Dry Beans, Eggs & Nuts Group

Vegetable Group

Fruit Group

Bread, Cereal, Rice & Pasta Group

And other carbohydrates

Water

Time	Food Eaten & Quantity	Why You Ate?	Calories	Fat
	Hours Between Snack & Bedtime	Total For Day=		

Work Out

Aerobic Activity

Strength Training

Flexibility

Activity	light / moderate / hard
Time/Distance	1 2 3 4 5

How I Felt Today...

Wednesday _____

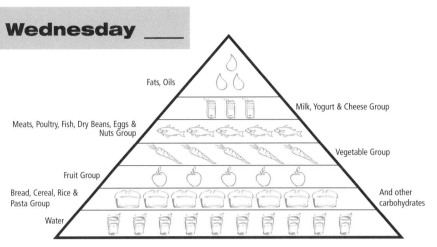

Fats, Oils

Milk, Yogurt & Cheese Group

Meats, Poultry, Fish, Dry Beans, Eggs & Nuts Group

Vegetable Group

Fruit Group

Bread, Cereal, Rice & Pasta Group

And other carbohydrates

Water

Time	Food Eaten & Quantity	Why You Ate?	Calories	Fat
	Hours Between Snack & Bedtime	Total For Day=		

Work Out

Aerobic Activity

Strength Training

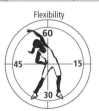

Flexibility

Activity	light / moderate / hard
Time/Distance	1 2 3 4 5

How I Felt Today...

Thursday _____

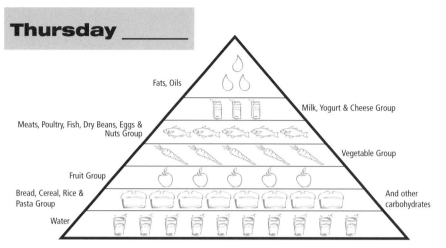

Fats, Oils

Milk, Yogurt & Cheese Group

Meats, Poultry, Fish, Dry Beans, Eggs & Nuts Group

Vegetable Group

Fruit Group

Bread, Cereal, Rice & Pasta Group

And other carbohydrates

Water

Time	Food Eaten & Quantity	Why You Ate?	Calories	Fat
	Hours Between Snack & Bedtime	Total For Day=		

Work Out

Aerobic Activity

Strength Training

Flexibility

Activity	light / moderate / hard
Time/Distance	1 2 3 4 5

How I Felt Today...

Friday _____

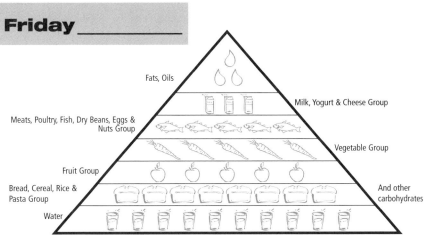

Fats, Oils

Milk, Yogurt & Cheese Group

Meats, Poultry, Fish, Dry Beans, Eggs & Nuts Group

Vegetable Group

Fruit Group

And other carbohydrates

Bread, Cereal, Rice & Pasta Group

Water

Time	Food Eaten & Quantity	Why You Ate?	Calories	Fat
	Hours Between Snack & Bedtime	Total For Day=		

Work Out

Aerobic Activity

Strength Training

Flexibility

Activity	light / moderate / hard
Time/Distance	1 2 3 4 5

How I Felt Today...

Saturday _____

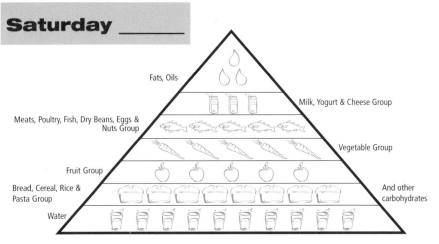

Fats, Oils

Milk, Yogurt & Cheese Group

Meats, Poultry, Fish, Dry Beans, Eggs & Nuts Group

Vegetable Group

Fruit Group

Bread, Cereal, Rice & Pasta Group

And other carbohydrates

Water

Time	Food Eaten & Quantity	Why You Ate?	Calories	Fat
	Hours Between Snack & Bedtime	Total For Day=		

Work Out

Aerobic Activity

Strength Training

Flexibility

Activity	light / moderate / hard
Time/Distance	1 2 3 4 5

How I Felt Today...

_____

_____

_____

_____

Sunday _____

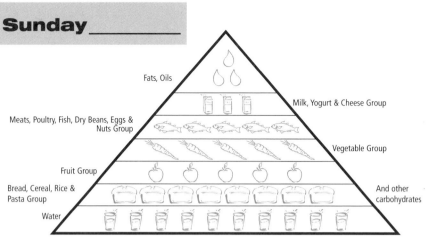

Fats, Oils

Milk, Yogurt & Cheese Group

Meats, Poultry, Fish, Dry Beans, Eggs & Nuts Group

Vegetable Group

Fruit Group

Bread, Cereal, Rice & Pasta Group

And other carbohydrates

Water

Time	Food Eaten & Quantity	Why You Ate?	Calories	Fat
	Hours Between Snack & Bedtime	Total For Day=		

Work Out

Aerobic Activity

Strength Training

Flexibility

Activity _____

Time/Distance _____

light / moderate / hard

1   2   3   4   5

How I Felt Today...

_____

_____

_____

_____

Fold

Weekly Recap

	M	T	W	Th	F	Sat	Sun	* Good √ Needs Work
Fat								
Dairy								
Protein								
Veggies								
Fruits								
Breads & Grains								
Water								

* = good   + = too much   - = not enough

Goals For Next Weeks Fuel:

_____

_____

_____

	M	T	W	Th	F	Sat	Sun	Total or Average For Week
Time Between Last Snack &Bedtime								
Cardio Sessions								
Strength Training Sessions								
Flexibility								
Abs								
Intensity Level								
Other								

Goals For Next Weeks Workout:

_____

_____

_____

Monday _____

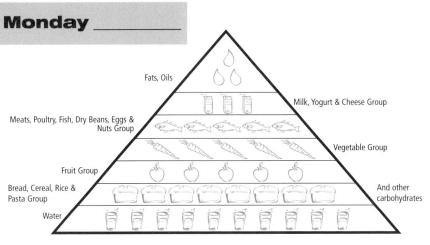

Fats, Oils

Milk, Yogurt & Cheese Group

Meats, Poultry, Fish, Dry Beans, Eggs & Nuts Group

Vegetable Group

Fruit Group

Fruit Group

Bread, Cereal, Rice & Pasta Group

And other carbohydrates

Water

Time	Food Eaten & Quantity	Why You Ate?	Calories	Fat
	Hours Between Snack & Bedtime	Total For Day=		

Work Out

Aerobic Activity

Strength Training

Flexibility

Activity	light / moderate / hard
Time/Distance	1 2 3 4 5

How I Felt Today...

Tuesday _____

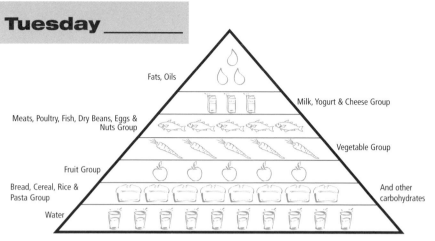

Fats, Oils

Milk, Yogurt & Cheese Group

Meats, Poultry, Fish, Dry Beans, Eggs & Nuts Group

Vegetable Group

Fruit Group

Bread, Cereal, Rice & Pasta Group

And other carbohydrates

Water

Time	Food Eaten & Quantity	Why You Ate?	Calories	Fat
	Hours Between Snack & Bedtime	Total For Day=		

Work Out

Aerobic Activity

Strength Training

Flexibility

Activity	light / moderate / hard
Time/Distance	1 2 3 4 5

How I Felt Today...

Wednesday ____

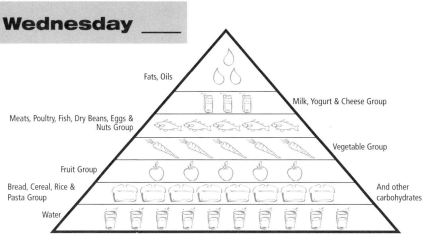

Time	Food Eaten & Quantity	Why You Ate?	Calories	Fat
Hours Between Snack & Bedtime		Total For Day=		

Work Out

Aerobic Activity

Strength Training

Flexibility

Activity	light / moderate / hard
Time/Distance	1 2 3 4 5

How I Felt Today...

Thursday _____

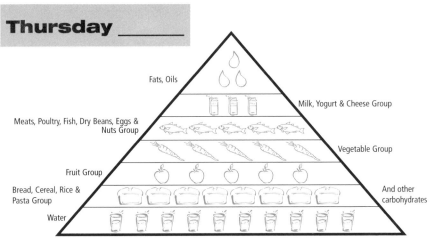

Time	Food Eaten & Quantity	Why You Ate?	Calories	Fat
	Hours Between Snack & Bedtime	Total For Day=		

Work Out

Aerobic Activity

Strength Training

Flexibility

Activity	light / moderate / hard
Time/Distance	1 2 3 4 5

How I Felt Today...

_____

_____

_____

_____

Friday _____

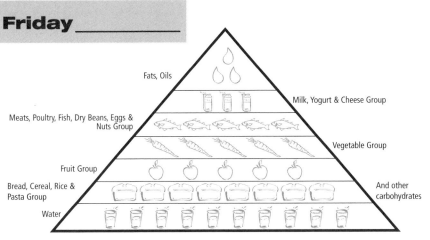

Fats, Oils

Milk, Yogurt & Cheese Group

Meats, Poultry, Fish, Dry Beans, Eggs & Nuts Group

Vegetable Group

Fruit Group

Bread, Cereal, Rice & Pasta Group

And other carbohydrates

Water

Time	Food Eaten & Quantity	Why You Ate?	Calories	Fat
	Hours Between Snack & Bedtime	Total For Day=		

Work Out

Aerobic Activity

Strength Training

Flexibility

Activity _____

Time/Distance _____

light / moderate / hard

1   2   3   4   5

How I Felt Today...

_____

_____

_____

_____

Saturday _____

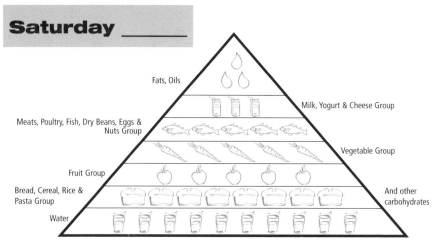

Fats, Oils

Milk, Yogurt & Cheese Group

Meats, Poultry, Fish, Dry Beans, Eggs & Nuts Group

Vegetable Group

Fruit Group

Bread, Cereal, Rice & Pasta Group

And other carbohydrates

Water

Time	Food Eaten & Quantity	Why You Ate?	Calories	Fat
	Hours Between Snack & Bedtime	Total For Day=		

Work Out

Aerobic Activity

Strength Training

Flexibility

Activity		light / moderate / hard
Time/Distance		1 2 3 4 5

How I Felt Today...

_____

_____

_____

_____

Sunday _____

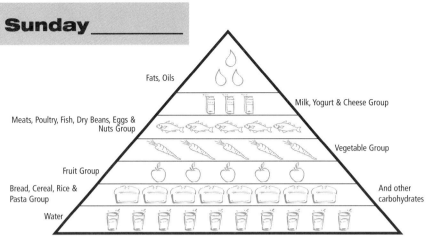

Time	Food Eaten & Quantity	Why You Ate?	Calories	Fat
	Hours Between Snack & Bedtime	Total For Day=		

Work Out

Aerobic Activity

Strength Training

Flexibility

Activity	light / moderate / hard
Time/Distance	1 2 3 4 5

How I Felt Today...

_____
_____
_____
_____

Weekly Recap

	M	T	W	Th	F	Sat	Sun	* Good √ Needs Work
Fat								
Dairy								
Protein								
Veggies								
Fruits								
Breads & Grains								
Water								

* = good   + = too much   - = not enough

Goals For Next Weeks Fuel:

_____

_____

_____

	M	T	W	Th	F	Sat	Sun	Total or Average For Week
Time Between Last Snack &Bedtime								
Cardio Sessions								
Strength Training Sessions								
Flexibility								
Abs								
Intensity Level								
Other								

Goals For Next Weeks Workout:

_____

_____

_____

Four Week Recap

Fold

	Week 1	Week 2	Week 3	Week 4	* Good √ Needs Work
Fat					
Dairy					
Protein					
Veggies					
Fruits					
Breads & Grains					
Water					

Goals For Next Four Weeks Fuel:

_____

_____

_____

	Week 1	Week 2	Week 3	Week 4	Average for 4 weeks
Average Time Between Last Snack & Bedtime					
Cardio Sessions					
Strength Training Sessions					
Flexibility					
Abs					
Average Intensity Level					
Other					

Goals For Next Four Weeks Workout:

_____

_____

_____

Mindful Quotes

▲ Keep moving, keep training, keep working out. Your body, with its amazing system of muscles, joints and bones, was meant to move. — Dr. Susan M. Kleiner

▲ The doctor of the future will give no medicine, but will interest his patient in the care of the human frame, in diet, and in the cause and prevention of disease.
— Thomas Edison

▲ Looking back on a good day is the ultimate pat-on-the-back. — Melody Biringer

▲ Old habits can't be thrown out the upstairs window. They have to be coaxed down the stairs one step at a time. — Mark Twain

▲ Physical fitness is not only one of the most important keys to a healthy body, it is the basis of dynamic and creative intellectual activity. The relationship between the soundness of the body and the activities of the mind is subtle and complex. Much is not yet understood. But we do know what the Greeks knew: that intelligence and skill can only function at the peak of their capacity when the body is healthy and strong; that hardy spirits and tough minds usually inhabit sound gods.
— John F. Kennedy

▲ Failure is the opportunity to begin again more intelligently. — Henry Ford

▲ People who cannot find time for recreation are obliged sooner or later to find time for illness. — John Wanamaker

▲ I know of no more encouraging fact than the unquestionable ability of man to elevate his life by conscious endeavor. — Henry David Thoreau

▲ It's just as easy to get used to and to enjoy eating foods that are good for you as it is to live on the health-robbing, high-fat, high-sugar, high-salt, high-calorie diet most Americans now consume. In fact, you can have your cake and eat it too, as long as it's not too much cake! — Jane Brody

▲ Setting a goal is not the main thing. It is deciding how you will go about achieving it and staying with that plan. — Tom Landry

Monday _____

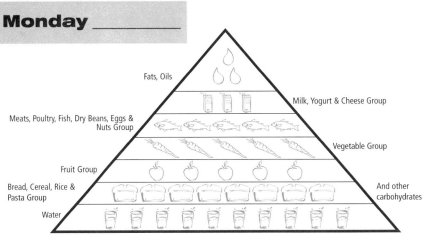

Fats, Oils

Milk, Yogurt & Cheese Group

Meats, Poultry, Fish, Dry Beans, Eggs & Nuts Group

Vegetable Group

Fruit Group

Bread, Cereal, Rice & Pasta Group

And other carbohydrates

Water

Time	Food Eaten & Quantity	Why You Ate?	Calories	Fat
	Hours Between Snack & Bedtime	Total For Day=		

Work Out

Aerobic Activity

Strength Training

Flexibility

Activity

Time/Distance

light / moderate / hard

1   2   3   4   5

How I Felt Today...

_____

_____

_____

_____

Tuesday _____

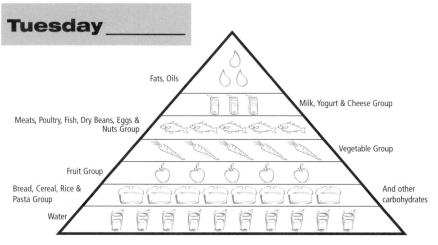

Fats, Oils

Milk, Yogurt & Cheese Group

Meats, Poultry, Fish, Dry Beans, Eggs & Nuts Group

Vegetable Group

Fruit Group

Bread, Cereal, Rice & Pasta Group

And other carbohydrates

Water

Time	Food Eaten & Quantity	Why You Ate?	Calories	Fat
	Hours Between Snack & Bedtime	Total For Day=		

Work Out

Aerobic Activity

Strength Training

Flexibility

Activity	light / moderate / hard
Time/Distance	1 2 3 4 5

How I Felt Today...

_____
_____
_____
_____

Wednesday ____

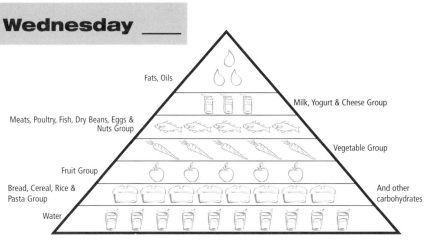

Time	Food Eaten & Quantity	Why You Ate?	Calories	Fat
	Hours Between Snack & Bedtime	Total For Day=		

Work Out

Activity _____   **light / moderate / hard**

Time/Distance _____   1   2   3   4   5

How I Felt Today... _____

_____

_____

_____

Thursday _____

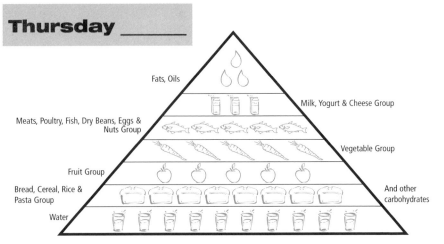

Fats, Oils

Milk, Yogurt & Cheese Group

Meats, Poultry, Fish, Dry Beans, Eggs & Nuts Group

Vegetable Group

Fruit Group

Bread, Cereal, Rice & Pasta Group

And other carbohydrates

Water

Time	Food Eaten & Quantity	Why You Ate?	Calories	Fat
	Hours Between Snack & Bedtime	Total For Day=		

Work Out

Aerobic Activity

Strength Training

Flexibility

Activity	light / moderate / hard
Time/Distance	1 2 3 4 5

How I Felt Today...

Friday _____

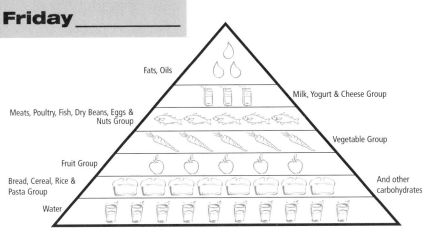

Time	Food Eaten & Quantity	Why You Ate?	Calories	Fat
	Hours Between Snack & Bedtime	Total For Day=		

Work Out

Aerobic Activity

Strength Training

Flexibility

Activity		light / moderate / hard
Time/Distance		1 2 3 4 5

How I Felt Today...

Saturday _____

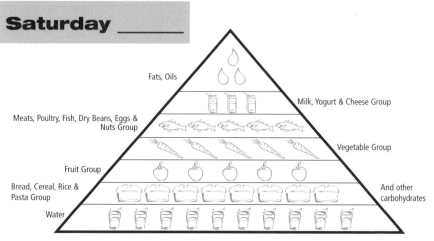

- Fats, Oils
- Milk, Yogurt & Cheese Group
- Meats, Poultry, Fish, Dry Beans, Eggs & Nuts Group
- Vegetable Group
- Fruit Group
- Bread, Cereal, Rice & Pasta Group
- And other carbohydrates
- Water

Time	Food Eaten & Quantity	Why You Ate?	Calories	Fat
	Hours Between Snack & Bedtime	Total For Day=		

Work Out

Aerobic Activity

Strength Training

Flexibility

Activity	light / moderate / hard
Time/Distance	1 2 3 4 5

How I Felt Today...

_____
_____
_____
_____

Sunday _____

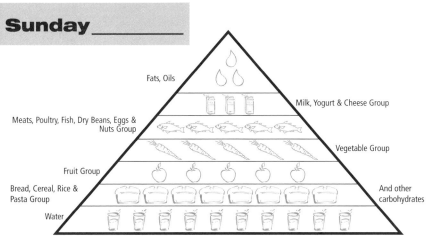

Time	Food Eaten & Quantity	Why You Ate?	Calories	Fat
	Hours Between Snack & Bedtime	Total For Day=		

Work Out

Aerobic Activity   Strength Training   Flexibility

Activity		light / moderate / hard
Time/Distance		1 2 3 4 5

How I Felt Today...

Weekly Recap

	M	T	W	Th	F	Sat	Sun	* Good √ Needs Work
Fat								
Dairy								
Protein								
Veggies								
Fruits								
Breads & Grains								
Water								

       * = good   + = too much   - = not enough

Goals For Next Weeks Fuel:

_____

_____

_____

	M	T	W	Th	F	Sat	Sun	Total or Average For Week
Time Between Last Snack &Bedtime								
Cardio Sessions								
Strength Training Sessions								
Flexibility								
Abs								
Intensity Level								
Other								

Goals For Next Weeks Workout:

_____

_____

_____

Monday _____

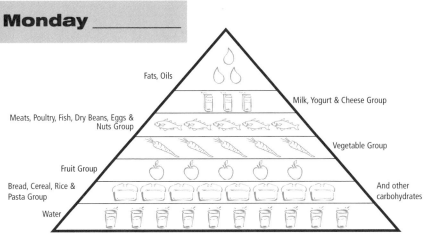

Time	Food Eaten & Quantity	Why You Ate?	Calories	Fat
	Hours Between Snack & Bedtime	Total For Day=		

Work Out

Aerobic Activity · Strength Training · Flexibility

Activity	light / moderate / hard
Time/Distance	1 2 3 4 5

How I Felt Today...

Tuesday _____

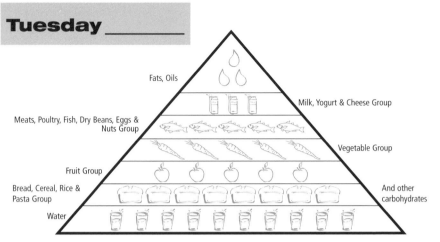

Fats, Oils

Milk, Yogurt & Cheese Group

Meats, Poultry, Fish, Dry Beans, Eggs & Nuts Group

Vegetable Group

Fruit Group

Bread, Cereal, Rice & Pasta Group

And other carbohydrates

Water

Time	Food Eaten & Quantity	Why You Ate?	Calories	Fat
	Hours Between Snack & Bedtime	Total For Day=		

Work Out

Aerobic Activity

Strength Training

Flexibility

Activity

Time/Distance

light / moderate / hard

1   2   3   4   5

How I Felt Today...

Wednesday _____

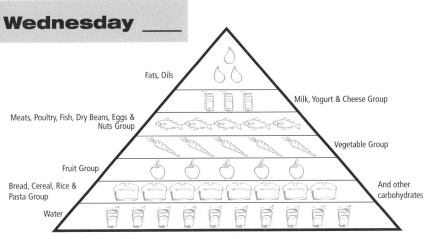

Fats, Oils

Milk, Yogurt & Cheese Group

Meats, Poultry, Fish, Dry Beans, Eggs & Nuts Group

Vegetable Group

Fruit Group

Bread, Cereal, Rice & Pasta Group

And other carbohydrates

Water

Time	Food Eaten & Quantity	Why You Ate?	Calories	Fat
	Hours Between Snack & Bedtime	Total For Day=		

Work Out

Aerobic Activity

60
45   15
30

Strength Training

Flexibility

60
45   15
30

Activity		light / moderate / hard
Time/Distance		1 2 3 4 5

How I Felt Today...

_____

_____

_____

_____

Thursday _____

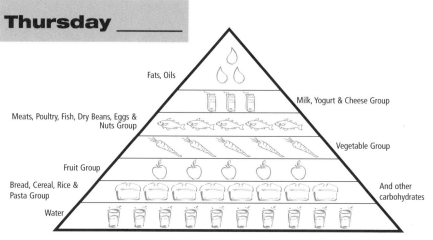

Fats, Oils

Milk, Yogurt & Cheese Group

Meats, Poultry, Fish, Dry Beans, Eggs & Nuts Group

Vegetable Group

Fruit Group

Bread, Cereal, Rice & Pasta Group

And other carbohydrates

Water

Time	Food Eaten & Quantity	Why You Ate?	Calories	Fat
	Hours Between Snack & Bedtime	Total For Day=		

Work Out

Aerobic Activity

Strength Training

Flexibility

Activity		light / moderate / hard
Time/Distance		1 2 3 4 5

How I Felt Today...

_____

_____

_____

_____

Friday _____

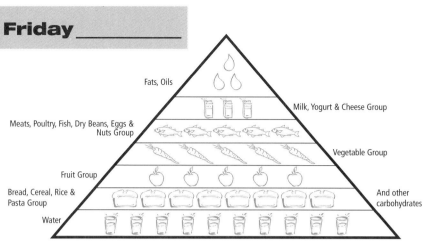

Time	Food Eaten & Quantity	Why You Ate?	Calories	Fat
	Hours Between Snack & Bedtime	Total For Day=		

Work Out

Aerobic Activity

Strength Training

Flexibility

Activity	light / moderate / hard
Time/Distance	1 2 3 4 5

How I Felt Today...

_____

_____

_____

_____

Saturday _____

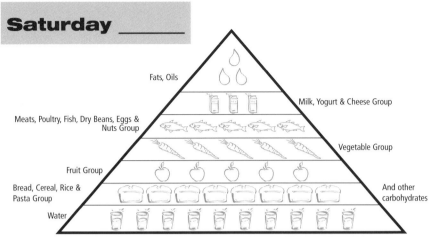

Fats, Oils

Milk, Yogurt & Cheese Group

Meats, Poultry, Fish, Dry Beans, Eggs & Nuts Group

Vegetable Group

Fruit Group

Bread, Cereal, Rice & Pasta Group

And other carbohydrates

Water

Time	Food Eaten & Quantity	Why You Ate?	Calories	Fat
	Hours Between Snack & Bedtime	Total For Day=		

Work Out

Aerobic Activity

Strength Training

Flexibility

Activity	light / moderate / hard
Time/Distance	1 2 3 4 5

How I Felt Today...

_____

_____

_____

_____

Sunday _____

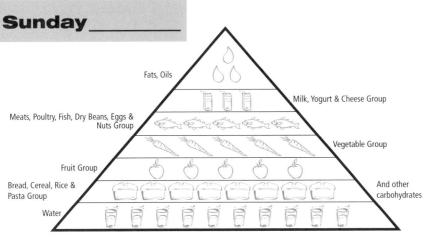

Fats, Oils

Milk, Yogurt & Cheese Group

Meats, Poultry, Fish, Dry Beans, Eggs & Nuts Group

Vegetable Group

Fruit Group

Bread, Cereal, Rice & Pasta Group

And other carbohydrates

Water

Time	Food Eaten & Quantity	Why You Ate?	Calories	Fat
	Hours Between Snack & Bedtime	Total For Day=		

Work Out

Aerobic Activity

Strength Training

Flexibility

Activity	light / moderate / hard
Time/Distance	1 2 3 4 5

How I Felt Today...

_____

_____

_____

_____

Weekly Recap

	M	T	W	Th	F	Sat	Sun	* Good √ Needs Work
Fat								
Dairy								
Protein								
Veggies								
Fruits								
Breads & Grains								
Water								

* = good   + = too much   - = not enough

Goals For Next Weeks Fuel:

_____

_____

_____

	M	T	W	Th	F	Sat	Sun	Total or Average For Week
Time Between Last Snack &Bedtime								
Cardio Sessions								
Strength Training Sessions								
Flexibility								
Abs								
Intensity Level								
Other								

Goals For Next Weeks Workout:

_____

_____

_____

Monday _____

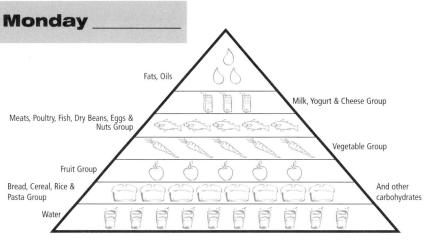

- Fats, Oils
- Milk, Yogurt & Cheese Group
- Meats, Poultry, Fish, Dry Beans, Eggs & Nuts Group
- Vegetable Group
- Fruit Group
- Bread, Cereal, Rice & Pasta Group
- And other carbohydrates
- Water

Time	Food Eaten & Quantity	Why You Ate?	Calories	Fat
	Hours Between Snack & Bedtime	Total For Day=		

Work Out

Aerobic Activity

Strength Training

Flexibility

Activity		light / moderate / hard
Time/Distance		1 2 3 4 5

How I Felt Today...

_____

_____

_____

_____

Tuesday _____

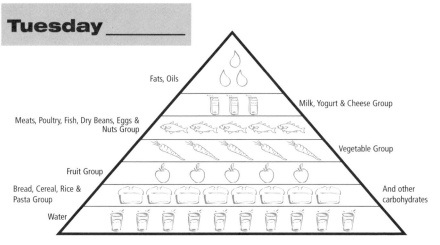

Fats, Oils

Milk, Yogurt & Cheese Group

Meats, Poultry, Fish, Dry Beans, Eggs & Nuts Group

Vegetable Group

Fruit Group

Bread, Cereal, Rice & Pasta Group

And other carbohydrates

Water

Time	Food Eaten & Quantity	Why You Ate?	Calories	Fat
	Hours Between Snack & Bedtime	Total For Day=		

Work Out

Aerobic Activity

Strength Training

Flexibility

Activity	light / moderate / hard
Time/Distance	1 2 3 4 5

How I Felt Today...

Wednesday ____

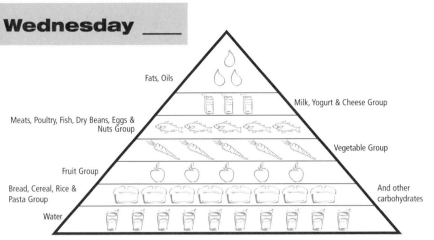

Time	Food Eaten & Quantity	Why You Ate?	Calories	Fat
	Hours Between Snack & Bedtime	Total For Day=		

Work Out

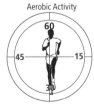

Aerobic Activity

Strength Training

Flexibility

Activity	light / moderate / hard
Time/Distance	1 2 3 4 5

How I Felt Today...

Thursday _____

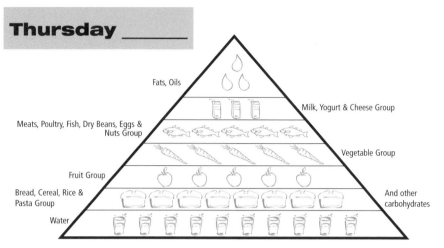

Time	Food Eaten & Quantity	Why You Ate?	Calories	Fat
	Hours Between Snack & Bedtime	Total For Day=		

Work Out

Aerobic Activity

Strength Training

Flexibility

Activity		light / moderate / hard
Time/Distance		1 2 3 4 5

How I Felt Today...

Friday _____

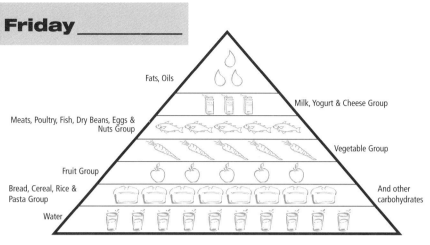

Time	Food Eaten & Quantity	Why You Ate?	Calories	Fat
	Hours Between Snack & Bedtime	Total For Day=		

Work Out

Aerobic Activity

Strength Training

Flexibility

Activity	light / moderate / hard
Time/Distance	1 2 3 4 5

How I Felt Today...

_____

_____

_____

_____

Saturday _____

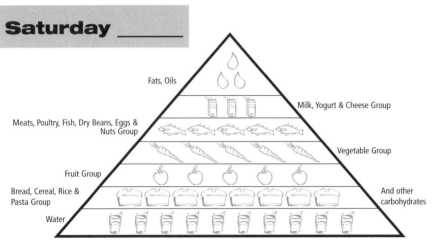

Fats, Oils

Milk, Yogurt & Cheese Group

Meats, Poultry, Fish, Dry Beans, Eggs & Nuts Group

Vegetable Group

Fruit Group

Bread, Cereal, Rice & Pasta Group

And other carbohydrates

Water

Time	Food Eaten & Quantity	Why You Ate?	Calories	Fat
	Hours Between Snack & Bedtime	Total For Day=		

Work Out

Aerobic Activity

Strength Training

Flexibility

Activity	light / moderate / hard
Time/Distance	1 2 3 4 5

How I Felt Today...

Sunday _____

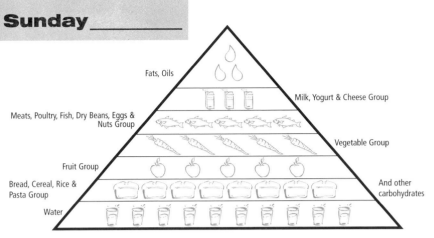

Time	Food Eaten & Quantity	Why You Ate?	Calories	Fat
	Hours Between Snack & Bedtime	Total For Day=		

Work Out

Aerobic Activity

Strength Training

Flexibility

Activity		light / moderate / hard
Time/Distance		1 2 3 4 5

How I Felt Today...

_____
_____
_____
_____

Weekly Recap

	M	T	W	Th	F	Sat	Sun	* Good √ Needs Work
Fat								
Dairy								
Protein								
Veggies								
Fruits								
Breads & Grains								
Water								

*　= good　　　+ = too much　　　- = not enough

Goals For Next Weeks Fuel:

_____

_____

_____

	M	T	W	Th	F	Sat	Sun	Total or Average For Week
Time Between Last Snack &Bedtime								
Cardio Sessions								
Strength Training Sessions								
Flexibility								
Abs								
Intensity Level								
Other								

Goals For Next Weeks Workout:

_____

_____

_____

Monday _____

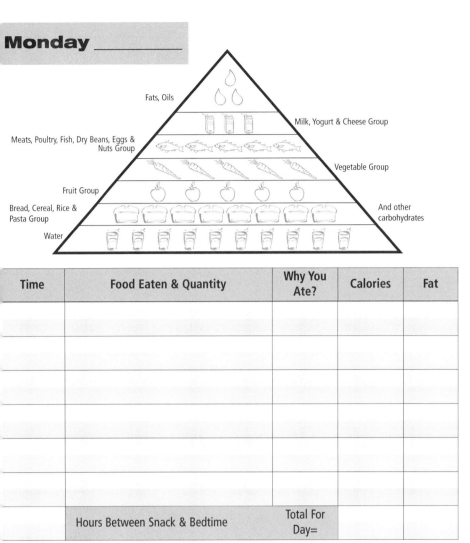

Fats, Oils

Milk, Yogurt & Cheese Group

Meats, Poultry, Fish, Dry Beans, Eggs & Nuts Group

Vegetable Group

Fruit Group

Bread, Cereal, Rice & Pasta Group

And other carbohydrates

Water

Time	Food Eaten & Quantity	Why You Ate?	Calories	Fat
	Hours Between Snack & Bedtime	Total For Day=		

Work Out

Aerobic Activity

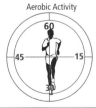

Strength Training

Flexibility

Activity	light / moderate / hard
Time/Distance	1 2 3 4 5

How I Felt Today...

Tuesday _____

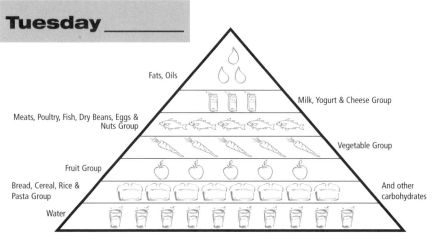

Fats, Oils

Milk, Yogurt & Cheese Group

Meats, Poultry, Fish, Dry Beans, Eggs & Nuts Group

Vegetable Group

Fruit Group

And other carbohydrates

Bread, Cereal, Rice & Pasta Group

Water

Time	Food Eaten & Quantity	Why You Ate?	Calories	Fat
	Hours Between Snack & Bedtime	Total For Day=		

Work Out

Aerobic Activity

Strength Training

Flexibility

Activity	light / moderate / hard
Time/Distance	1 2 3 4 5

How I Felt Today...

Wednesday _____

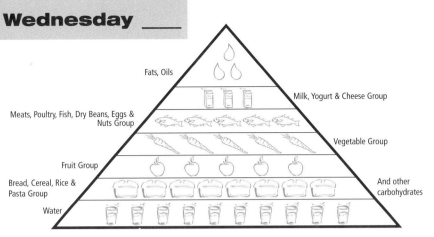

Fats, Oils

Milk, Yogurt & Cheese Group

Meats, Poultry, Fish, Dry Beans, Eggs & Nuts Group

Vegetable Group

Fruit Group

Bread, Cereal, Rice & Pasta Group

And other carbohydrates

Water

Time	Food Eaten & Quantity	Why You Ate?	Calories	Fat
	Hours Between Snack & Bedtime	Total For Day=		

Work Out

Aerobic Activity

Strength Training

Flexibility

Activity	light / moderate / hard
Time/Distance	1 2 3 4 5

How I Felt Today...

_____
_____
_____
_____

Thursday _____

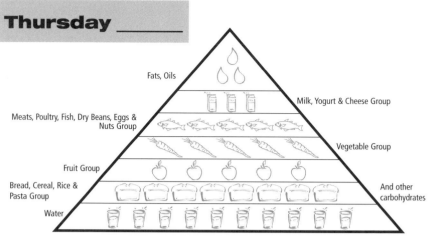

Time	Food Eaten & Quantity	Why You Ate?	Calories	Fat
	Hours Between Snack & Bedtime	Total For Day=		

Work Out

Aerobic Activity

Strength Training

Flexibility

Activity	light / moderate / hard
Time/Distance	1 2 3 4 5

How I Felt Today...

_____

_____

_____

_____

Friday _____

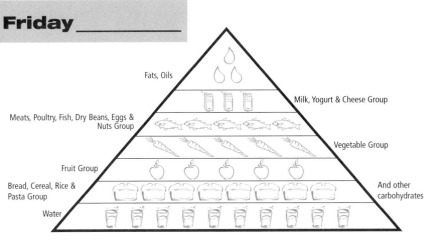

Time	Food Eaten & Quantity	Why You Ate?	Calories	Fat
	Hours Between Snack & Bedtime	Total For Day=		

Work Out

Aerobic Activity  Strength Training  Flexibility

Activity		light / moderate / hard
Time/Distance		1 2 3 4 5

How I Felt Today...

Saturday _____

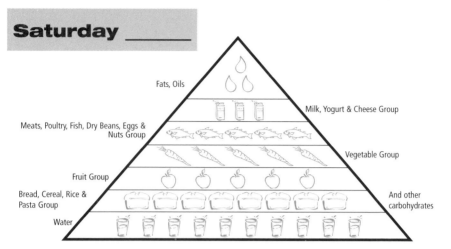

Fats, Oils

Milk, Yogurt & Cheese Group

Meats, Poultry, Fish, Dry Beans, Eggs & Nuts Group

Vegetable Group

Fruit Group

Bread, Cereal, Rice & Pasta Group

And other carbohydrates

Water

Time	Food Eaten & Quantity	Why You Ate?	Calories	Fat
	Hours Between Snack & Bedtime	Total For Day=		

Work Out

Aerobic Activity

Strength Training

Flexibility

Activity	light / moderate / hard
Time/Distance	1 2 3 4 5

How I Felt Today...

_____

_____

_____

_____

Sunday _____

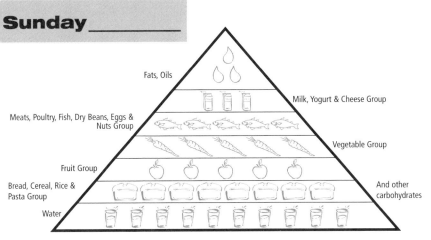

Fats, Oils

Milk, Yogurt & Cheese Group

Meats, Poultry, Fish, Dry Beans, Eggs & Nuts Group

Vegetable Group

Fruit Group

Bread, Cereal, Rice & Pasta Group

And other carbohydrates

Water

Time	Food Eaten & Quantity	Why You Ate?	Calories	Fat
	Hours Between Snack & Bedtime	Total For Day=		

Work Out

Aerobic Activity

Strength Training

Flexibility

Activity _____

Time/Distance _____

light / moderate / hard

1   2   3   4   5

How I Felt Today... _____

_____

_____

_____

Fold

Weekly Recap

	M	T	W	Th	F	Sat	Sun	*Good ✓ Needs Work
Fat								
Dairy								
Protein								
Veggies								
Fruits								
Breads & Grains								
Water								

* = good   + = too much   - = not enough

Goals For Next Weeks Fuel:

_____

_____

_____

	M	T	W	Th	F	Sat	Sun	Total or Average For Week
Time Between Last Snack &Bedtime								
Cardio Sessions								
Strength Training Sessions								
Flexibility								
Abs								
Intensity Level								
Other								

Goals For Next Weeks Workout:

_____

_____

_____

Four Week Recap

Fold

	Week 1	Week 2	Week 3	Week 4	* Good √ Needs Work
Fat					
Dairy					
Protein					
Veggies					
Fruits					
Breads & Grains					
Water					

Goals For Next Four Weeks Fuel:

_____

_____

_____

	Week 1	Week 2	Week 3	Week 4	Average for 4 weeks
Average Time Between Last Snack & Bedtime					
Cardio Sessions					
Strength Training Sessions					
Flexibility					
Abs					
Average Intensity Level					
Other					

Goals For Next Four Weeks Workout:

_____

_____

_____

Twelve Week Recap

	End Of Week 4	End Of Week 8	End Of Week 12	* Good √ Needs Work
Fat				
Dairy				
Protein				
Veggies				
Fruits				
Breads & Grains				
Water				

Fuel Recap:

	End Of Week 4	End Of Week 8	End Of Week 12	Average For 12 Weeks
Average Time Between Last Snack & Bedtime				
Cardio Sessions				
Strength Training Sessions				
Flexibility				
Abs				
Average Intensity Level				
Other				

Workout Recap: